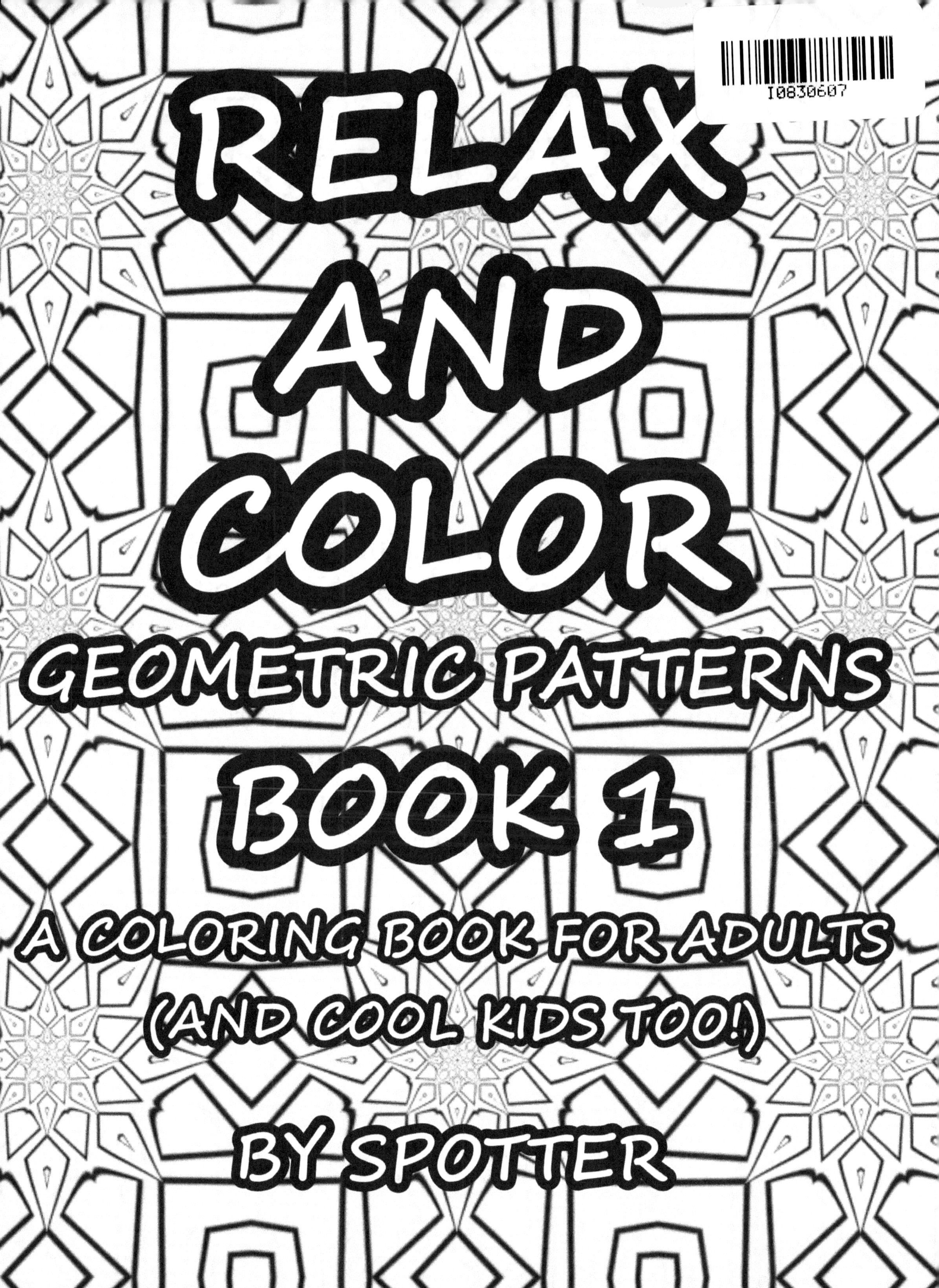

RELAX
AND
COLOR
GEOMETRIC PATTERNS
BOOK 1
A COLORING BOOK FOR ADULTS
(AND COOL KIDS TOO!)
BY SPOTTER

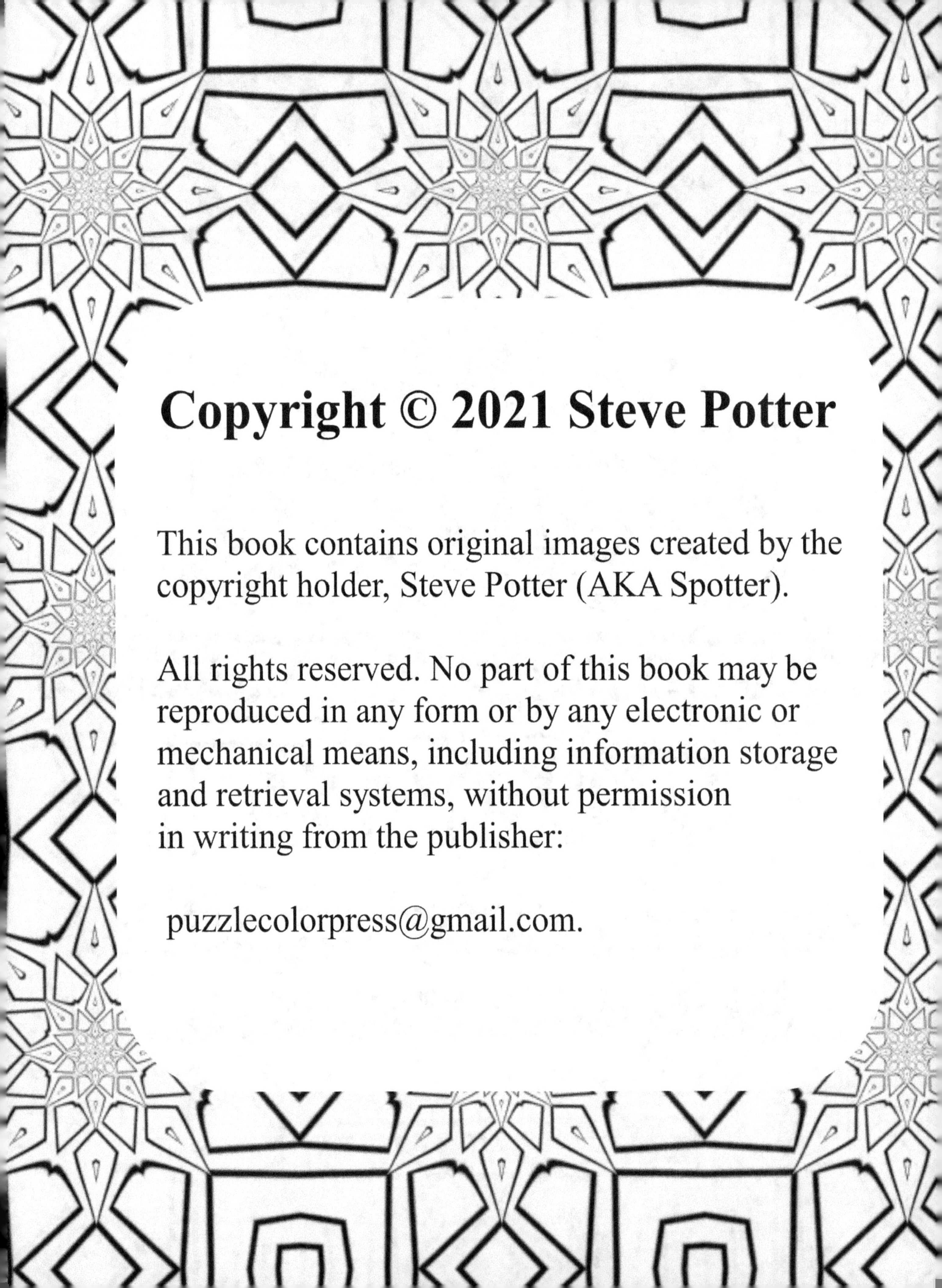

Copyright © 2021 Steve Potter

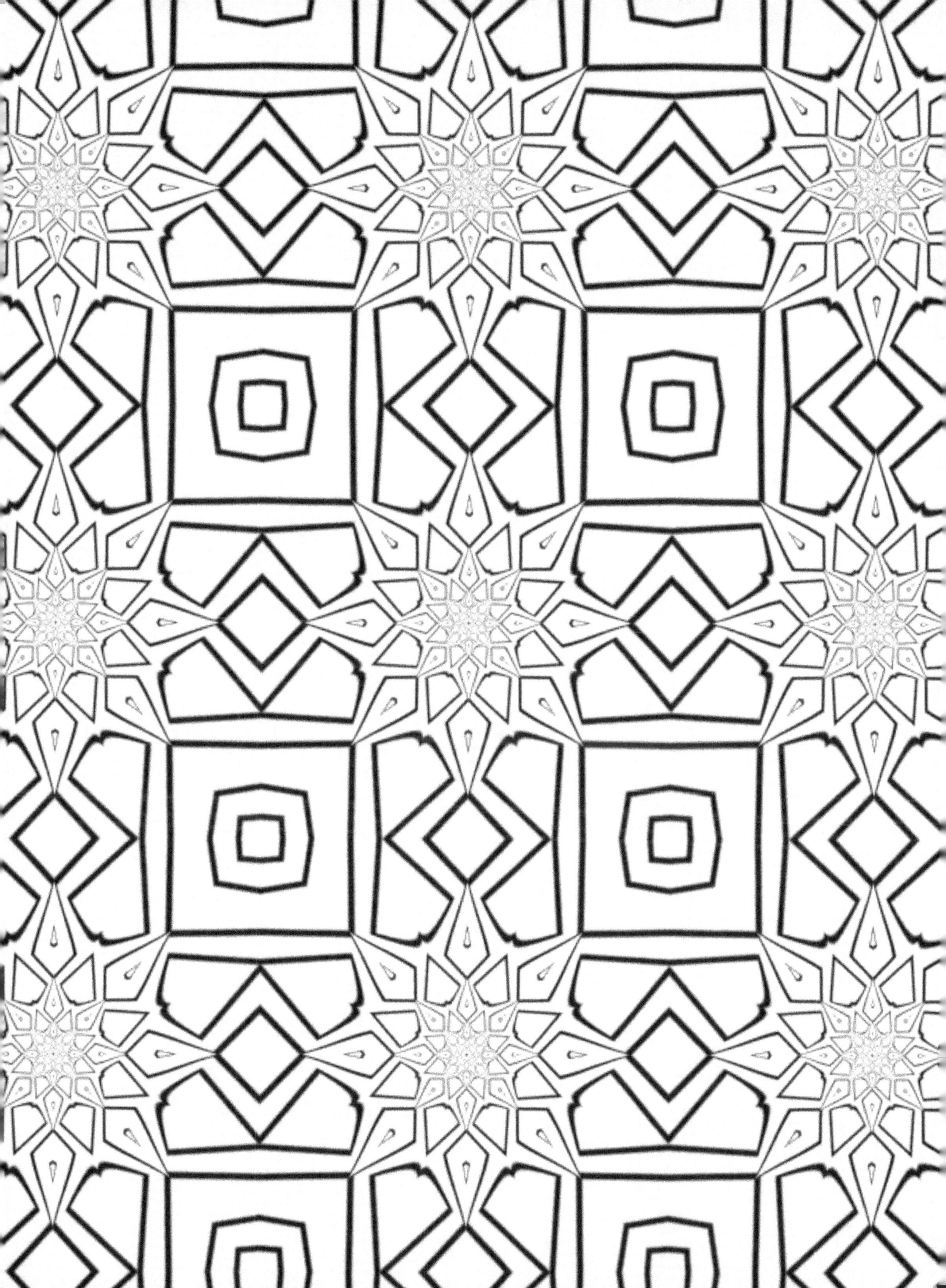

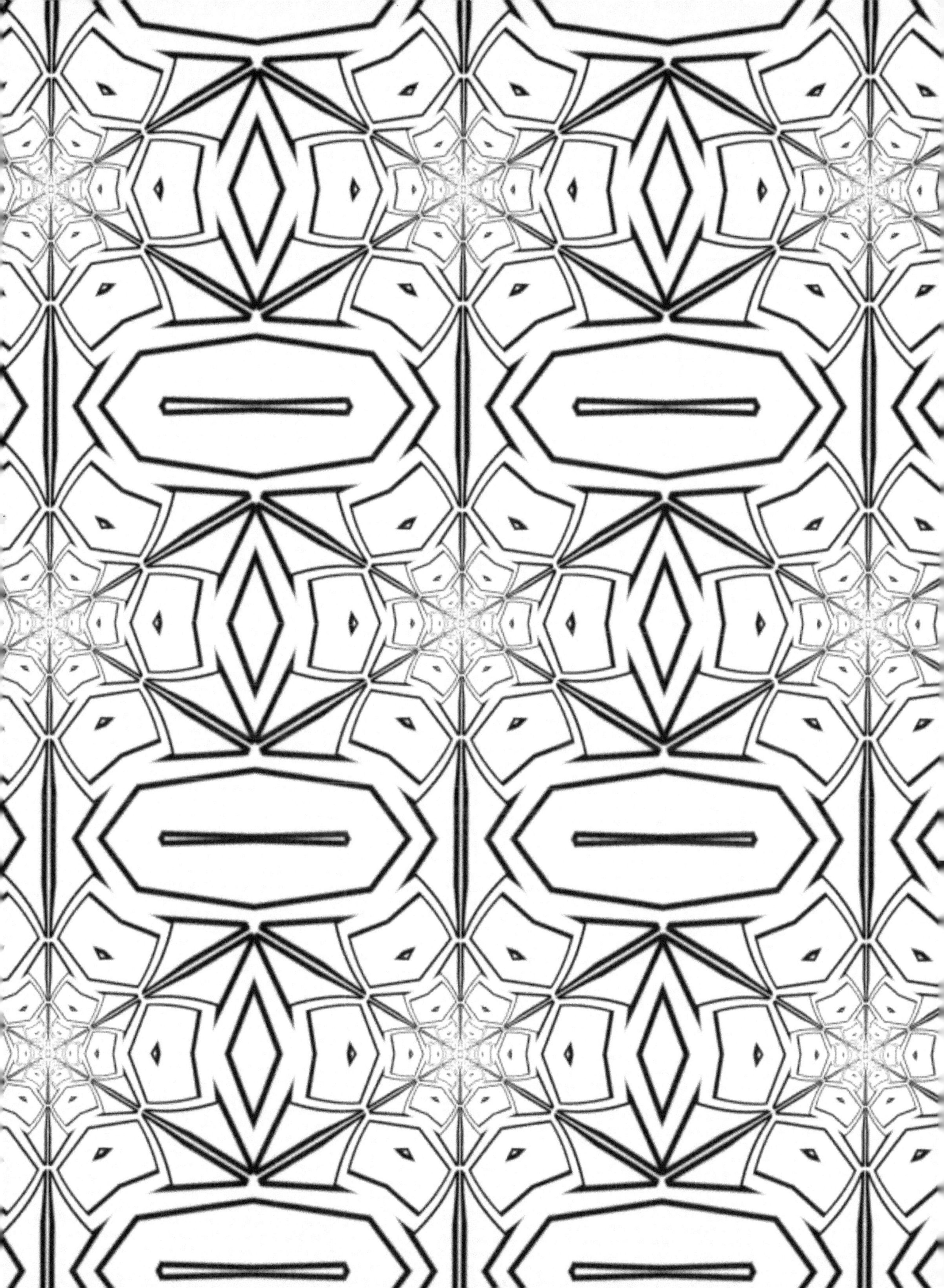

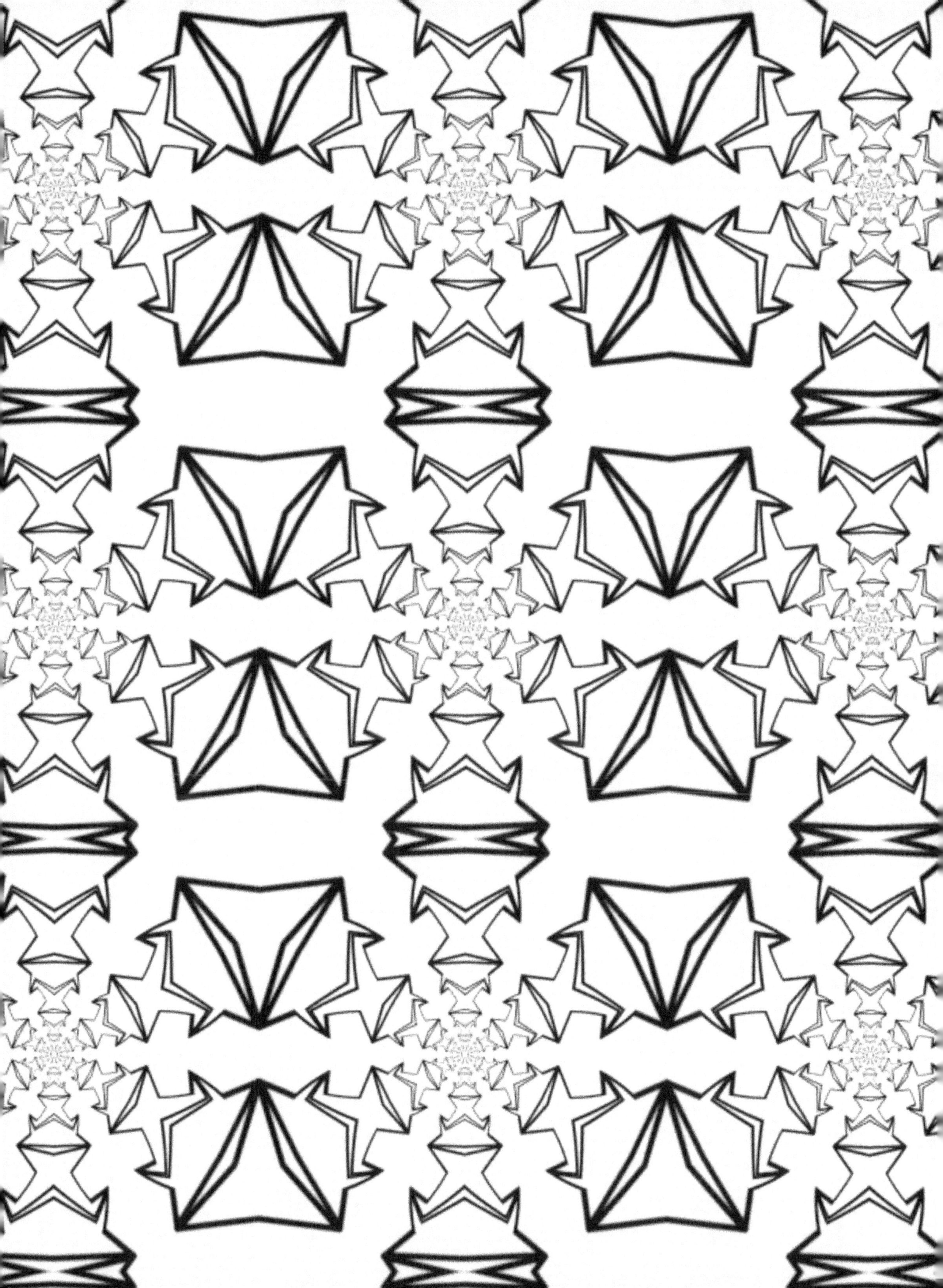

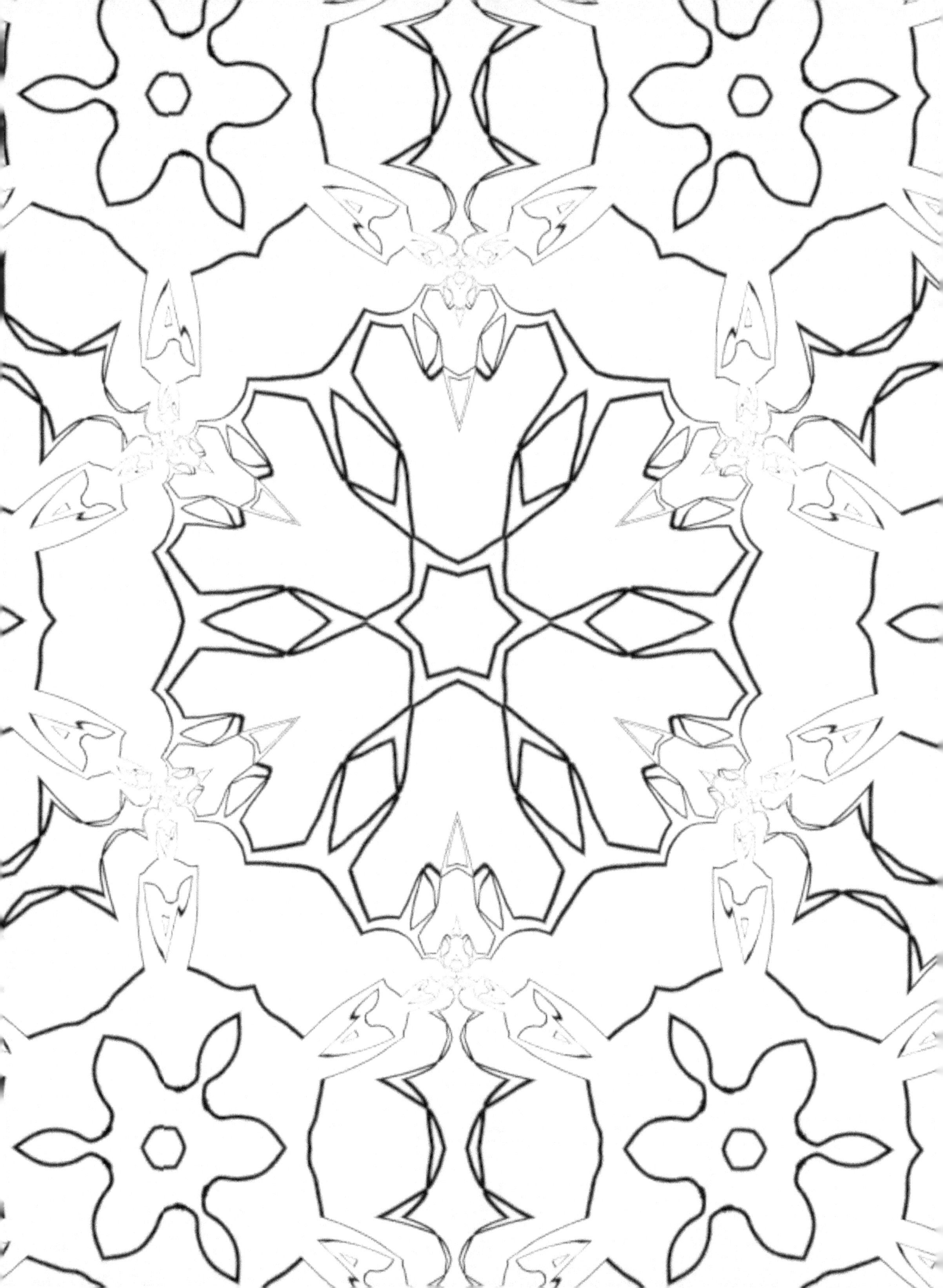

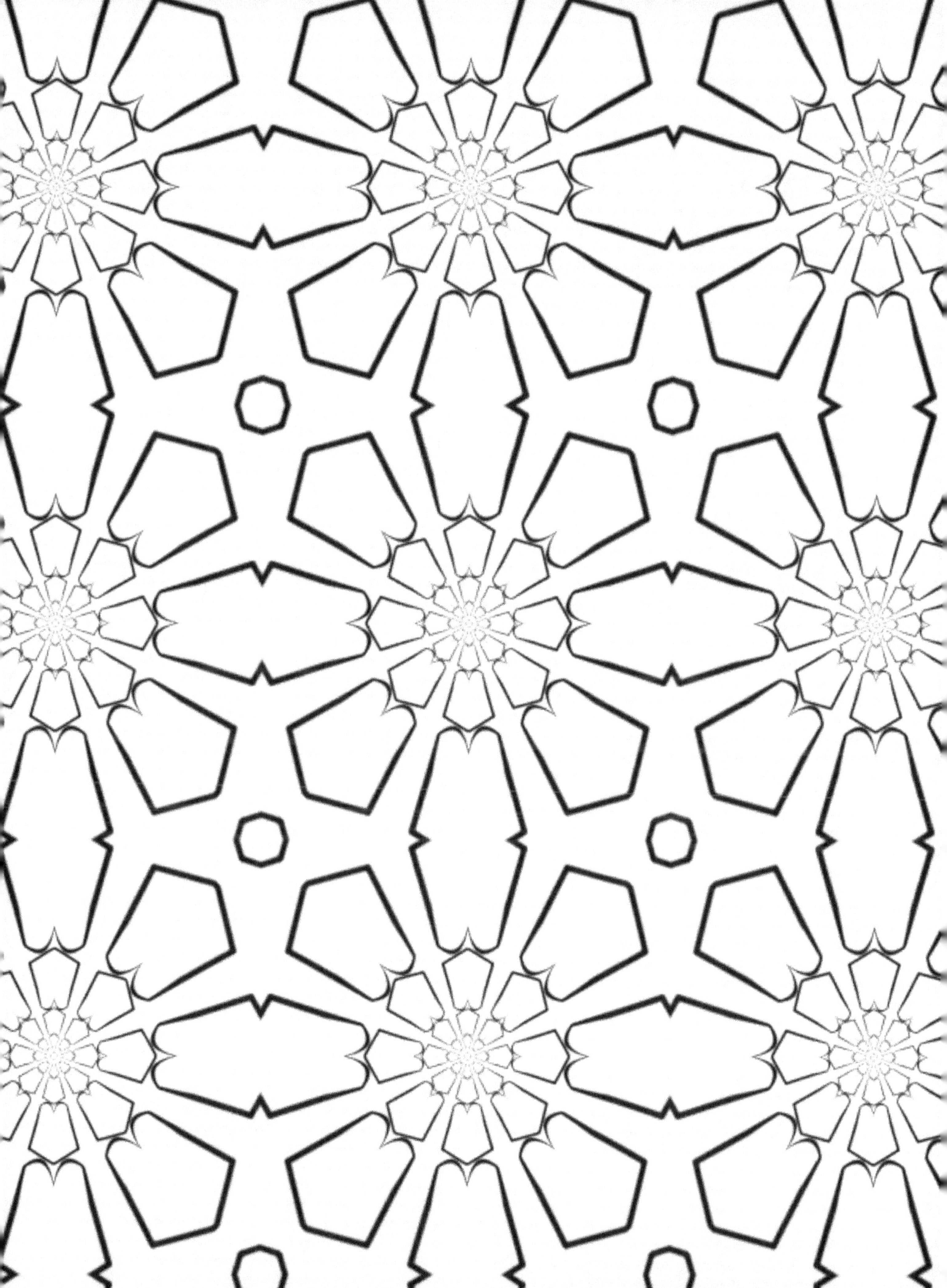

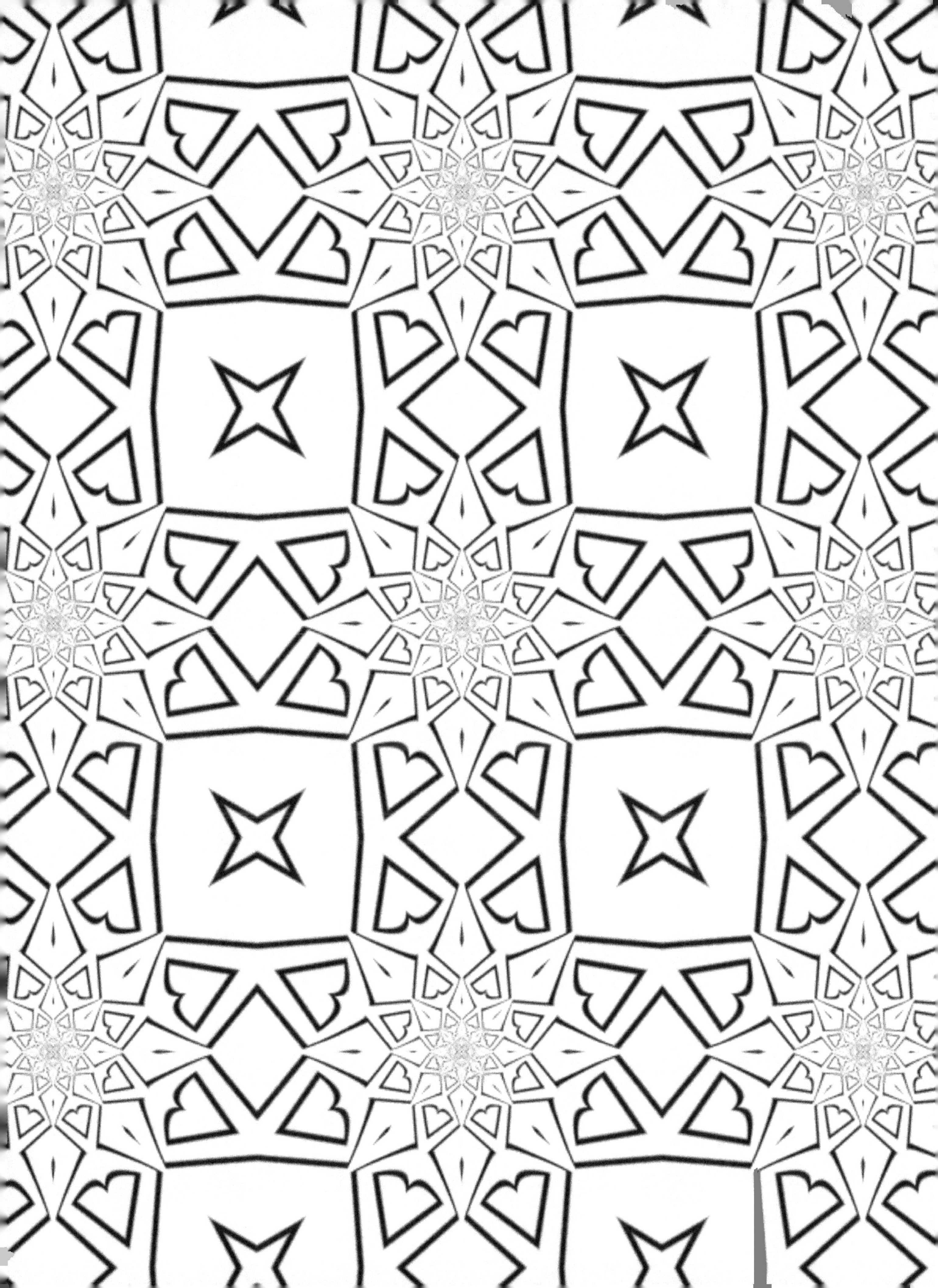

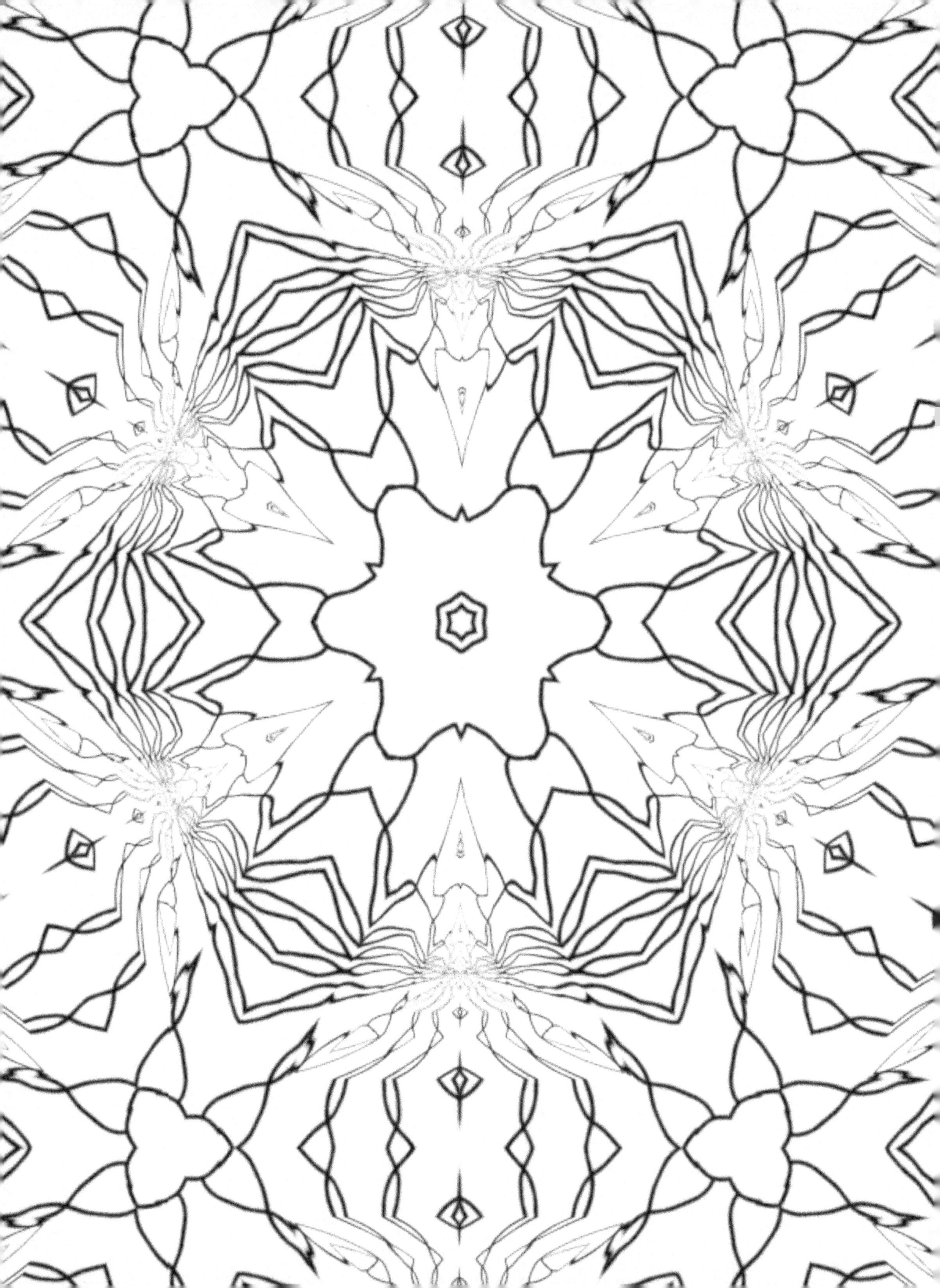

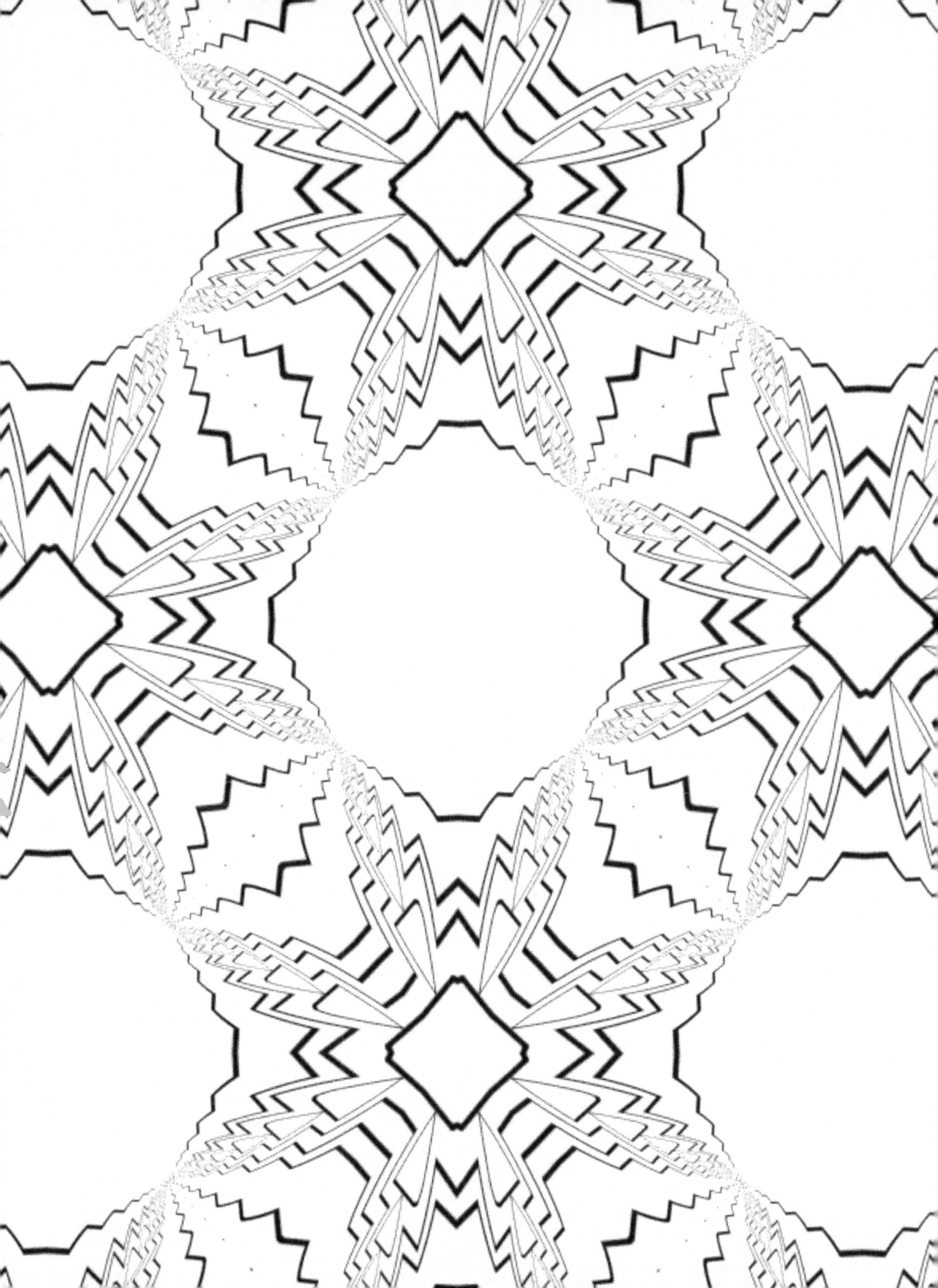

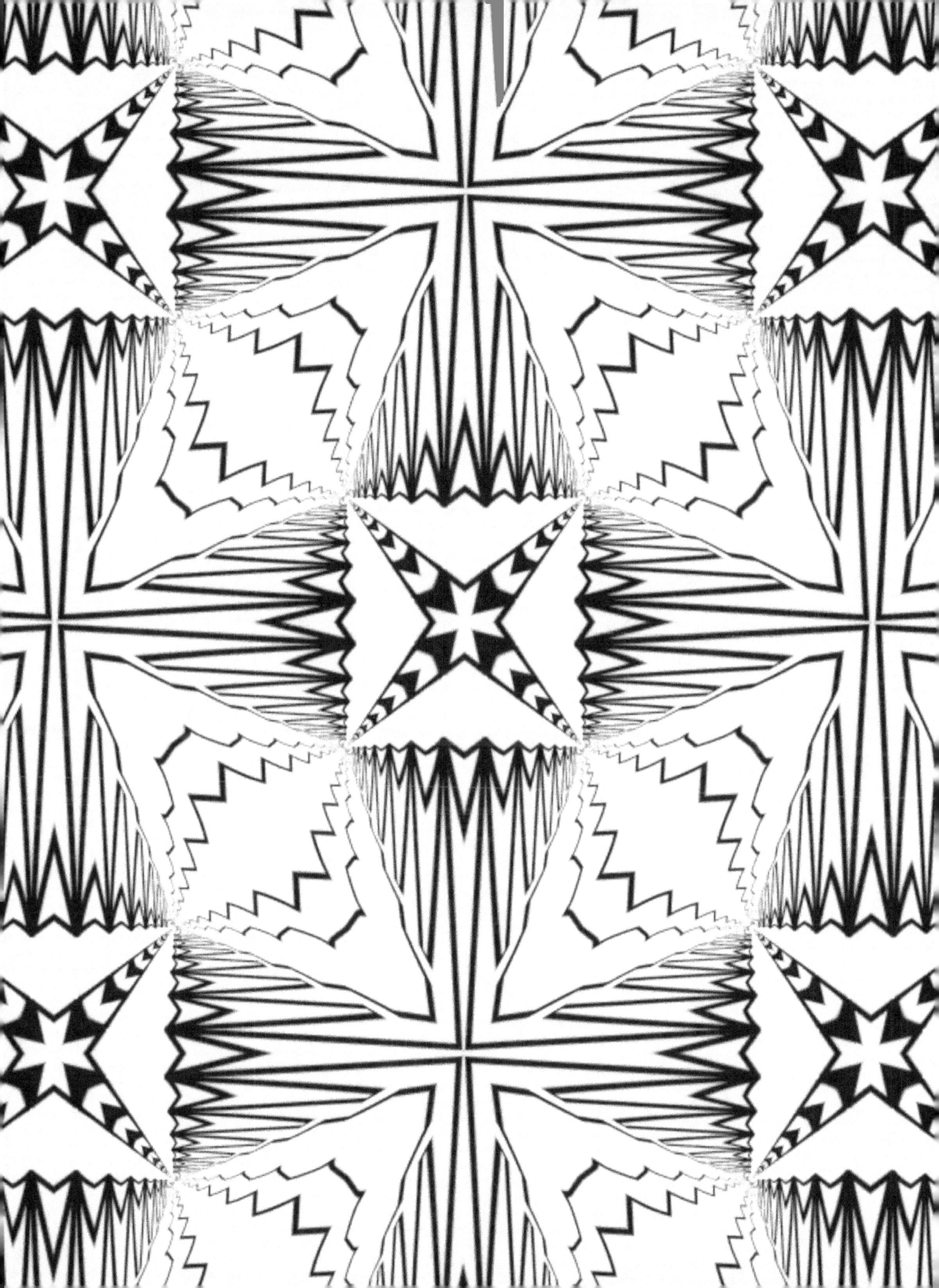

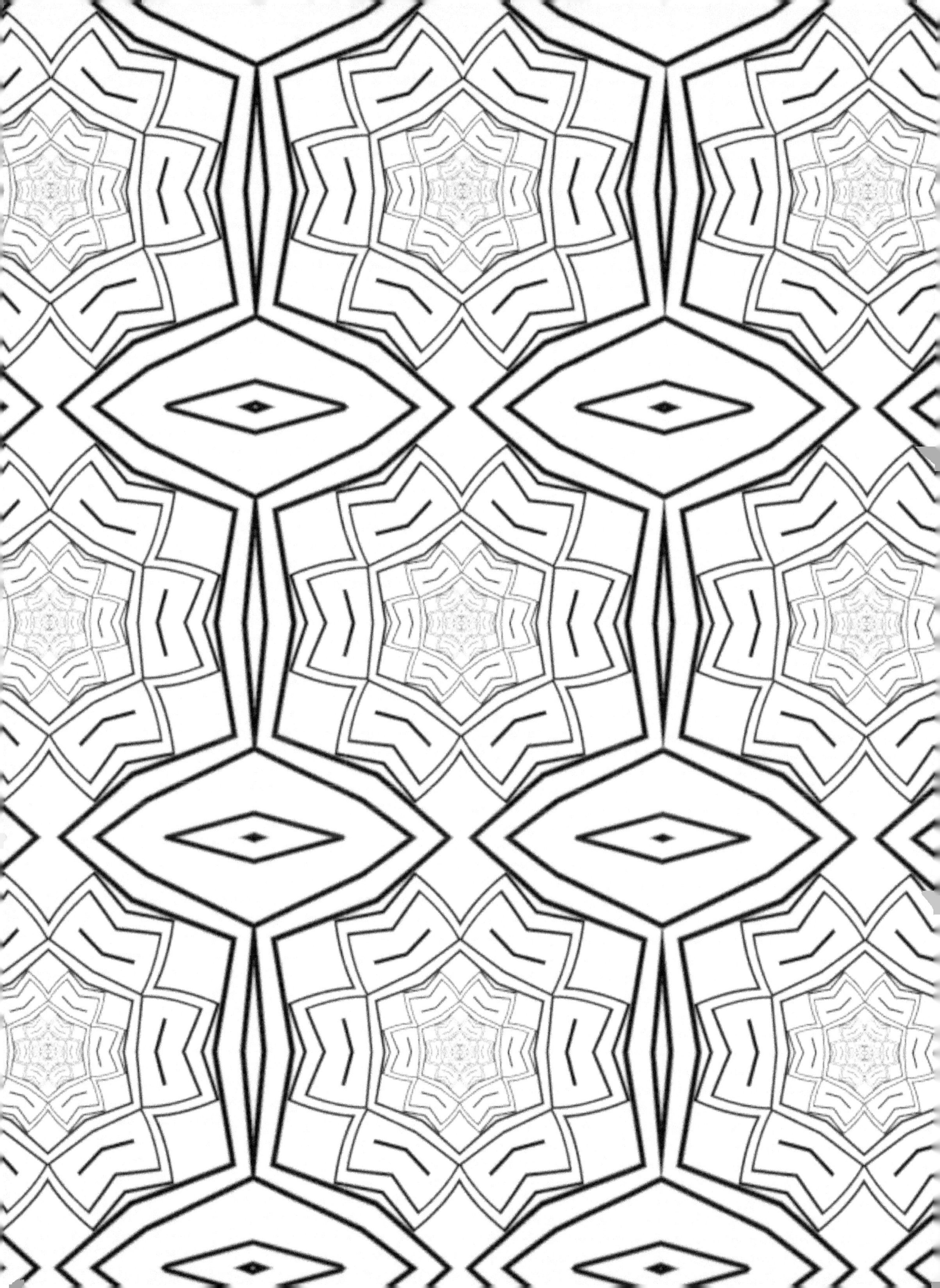

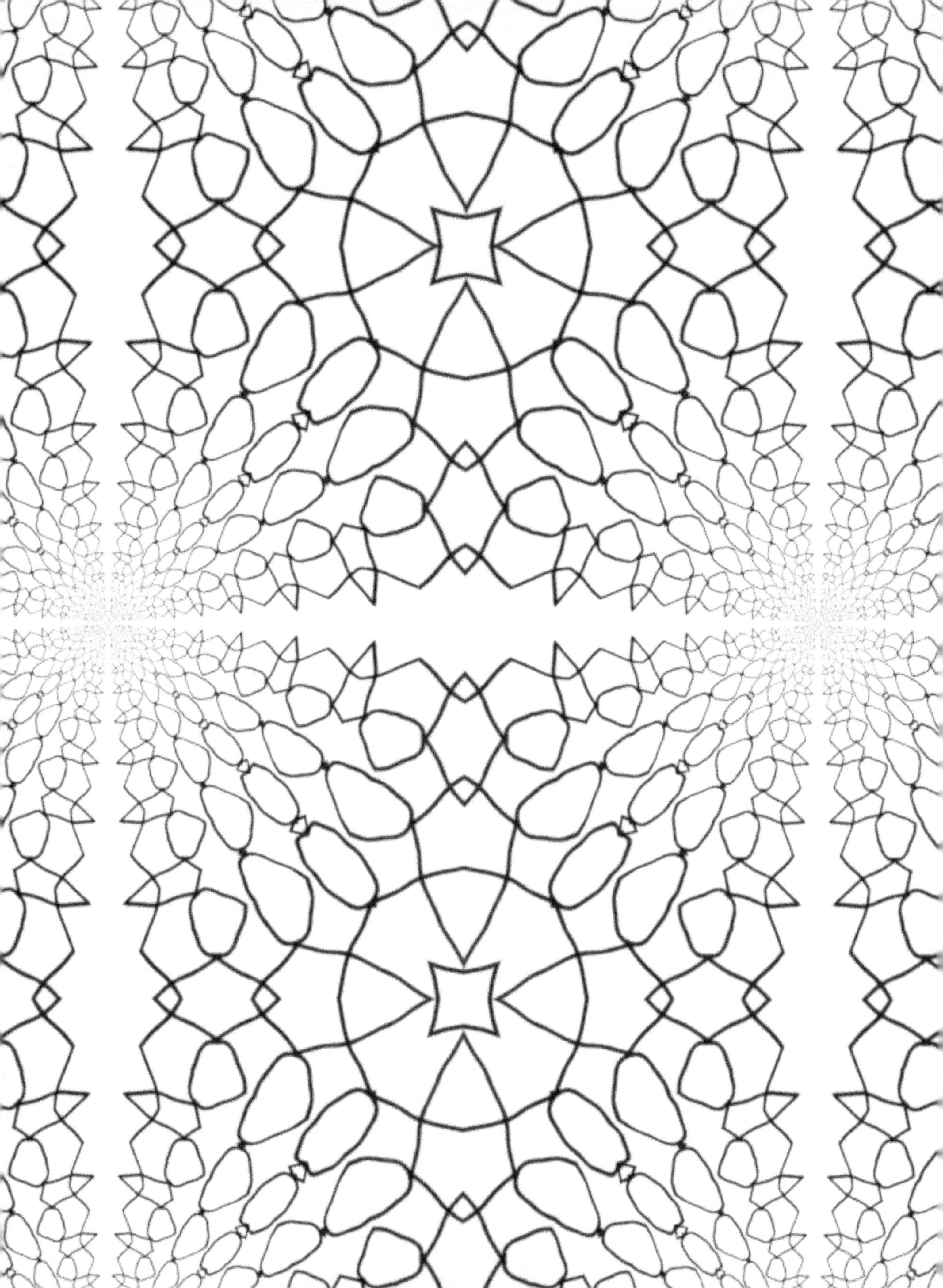

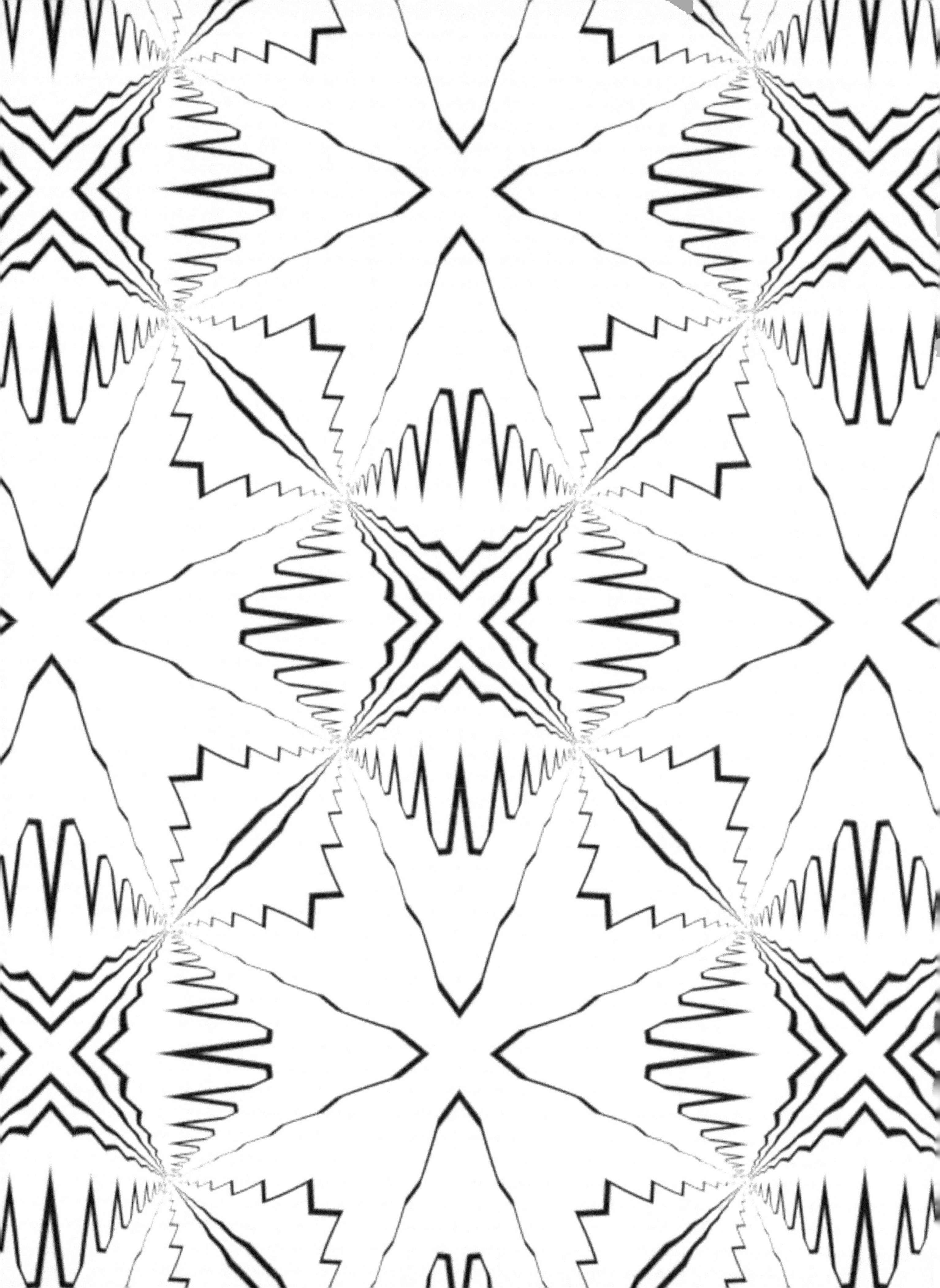

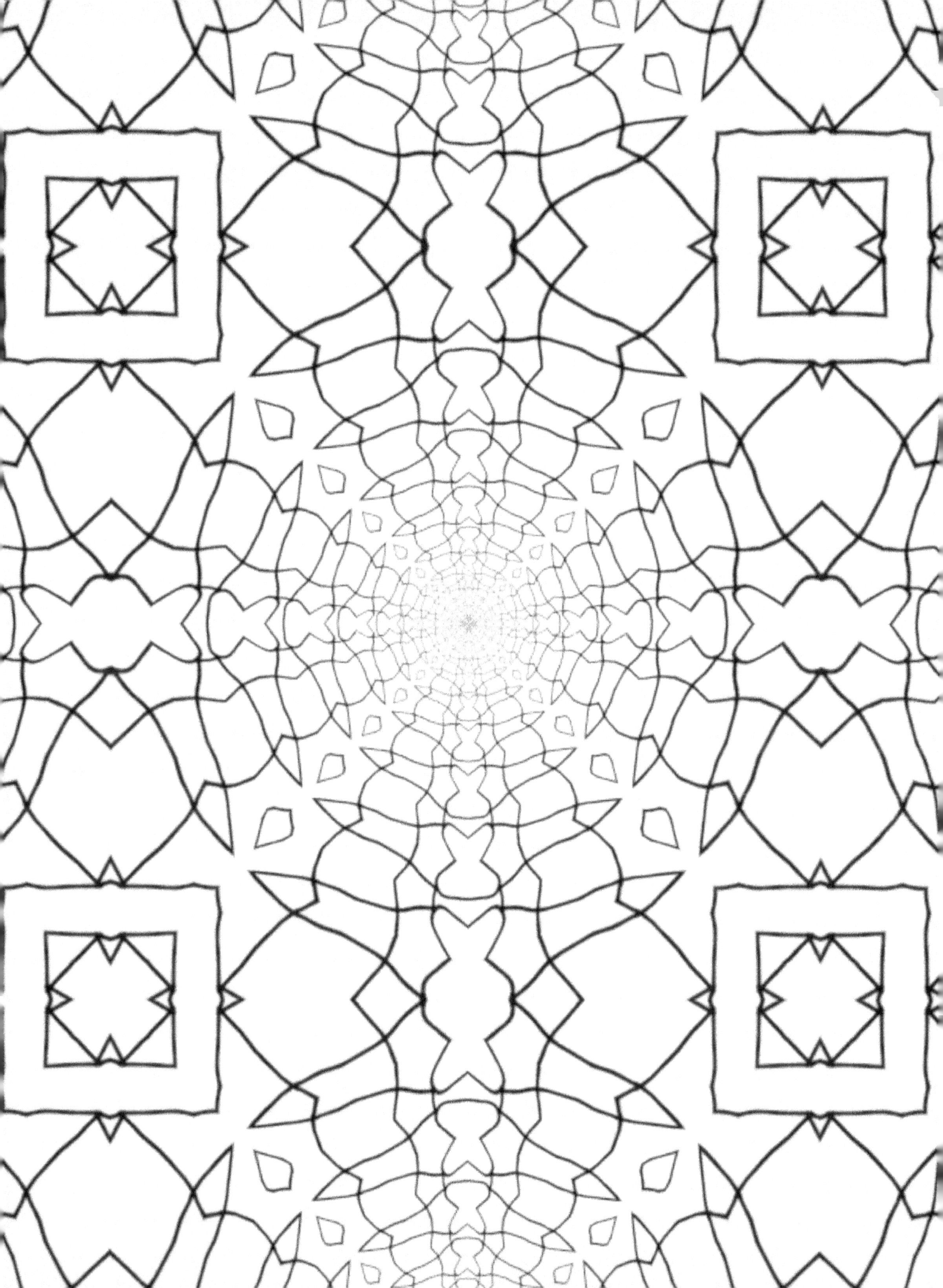

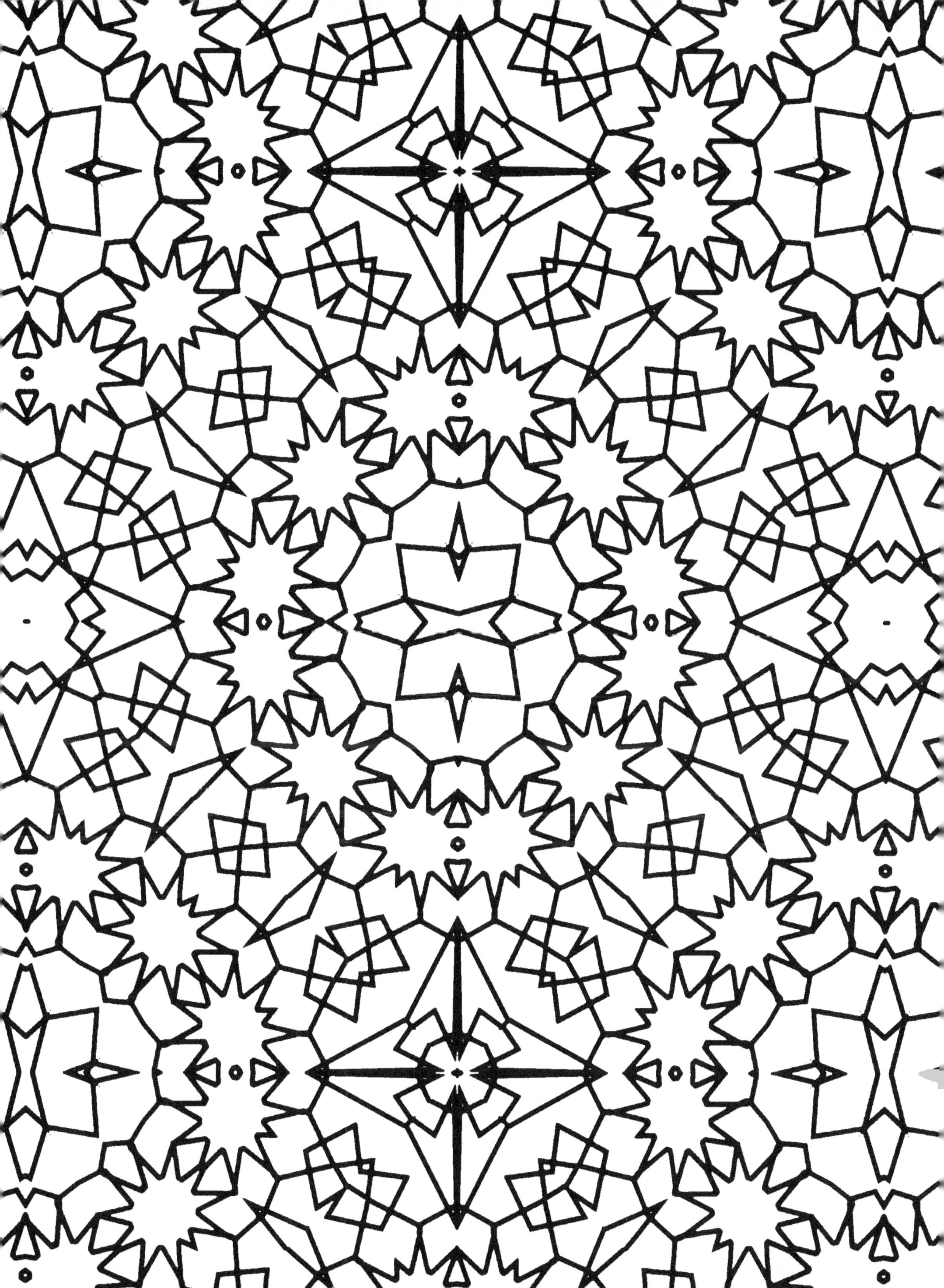

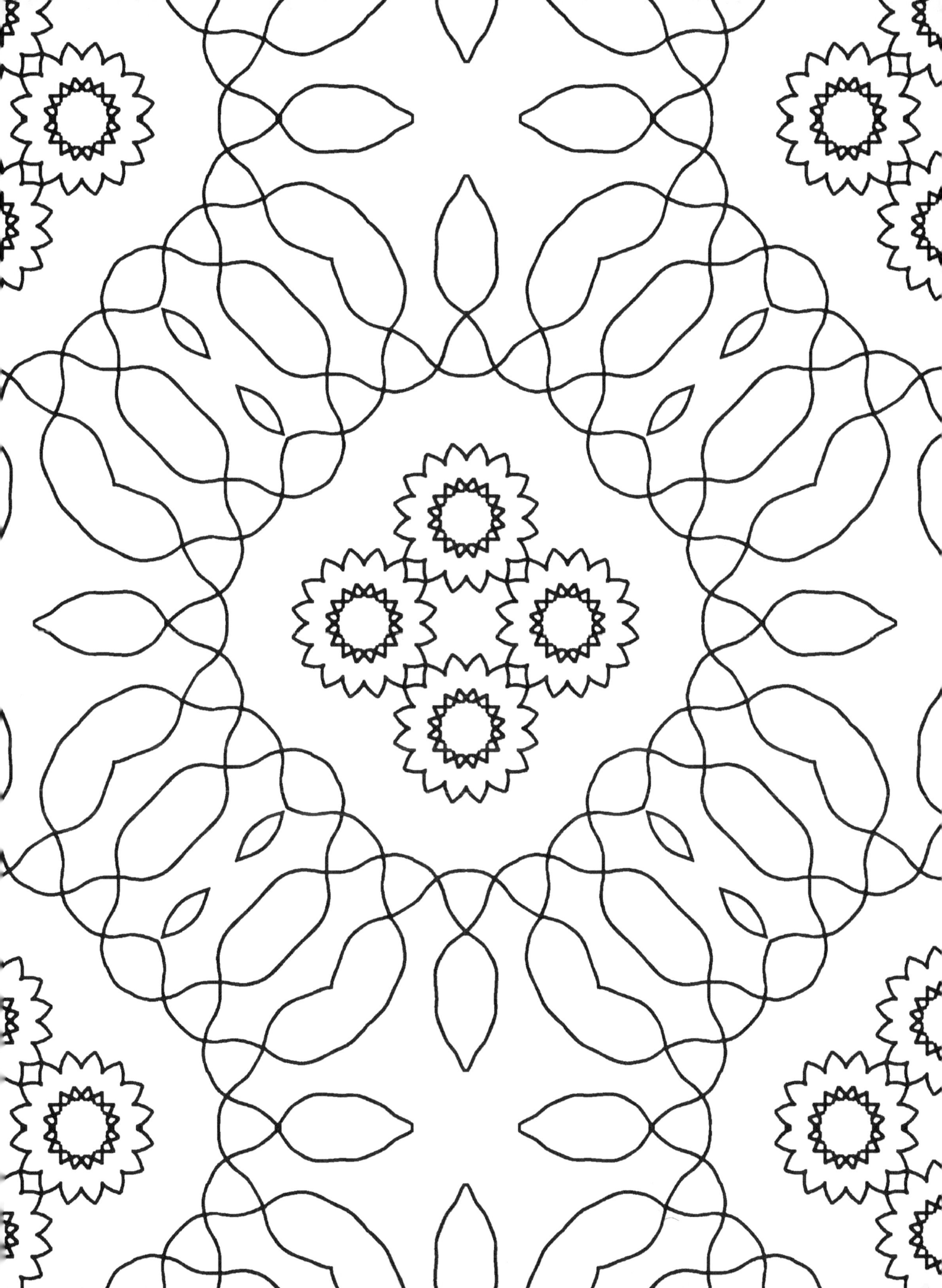

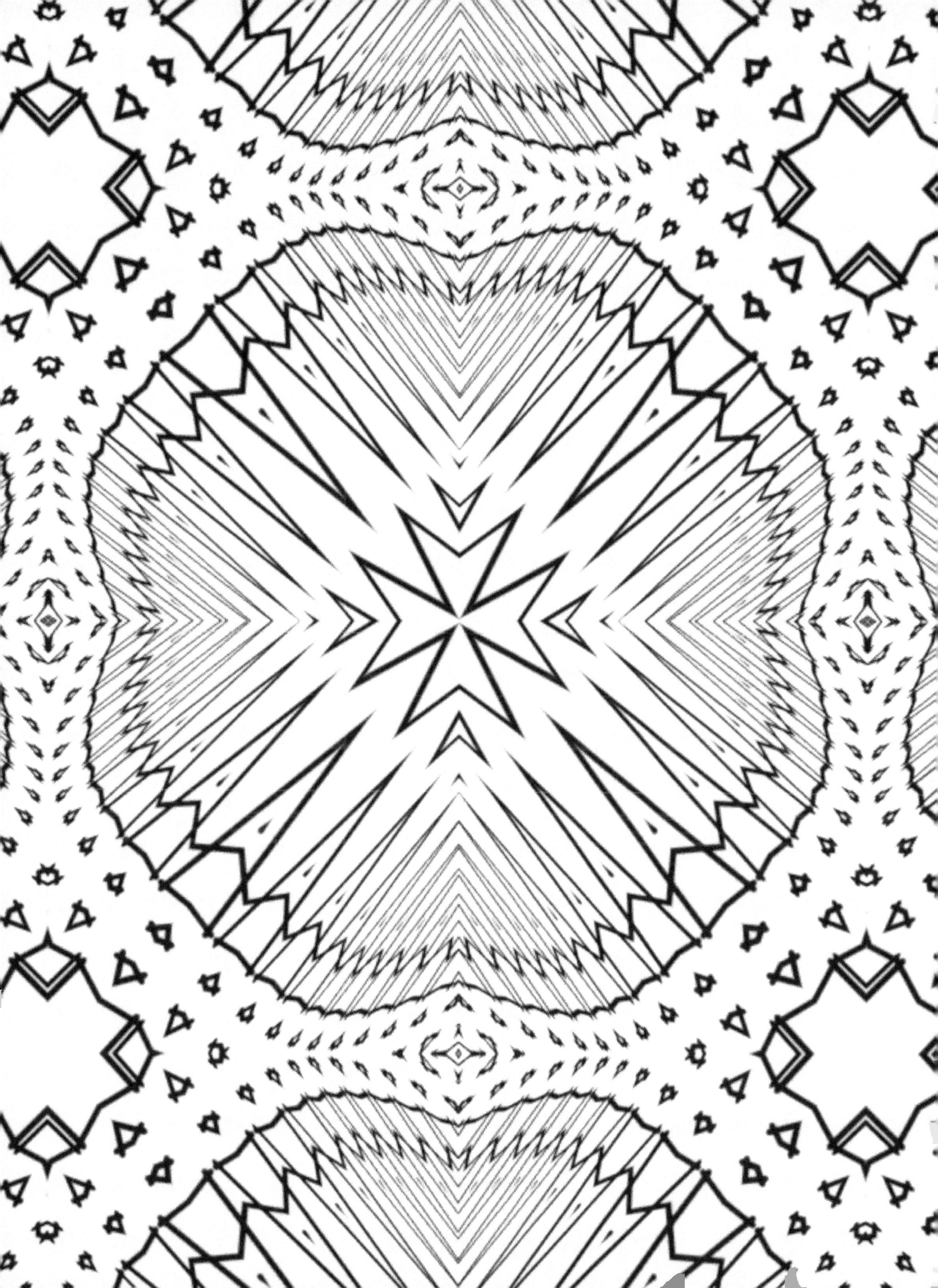

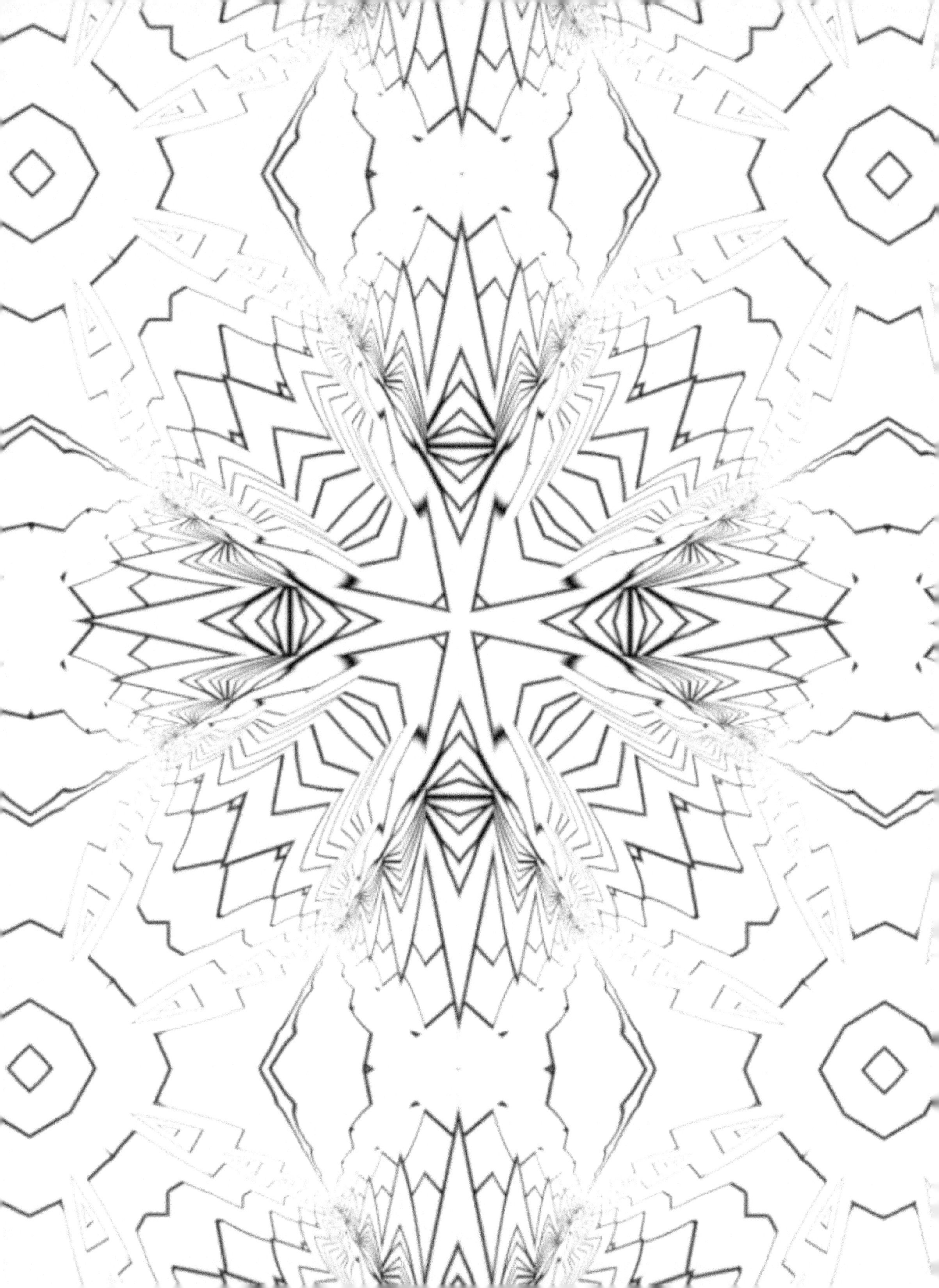

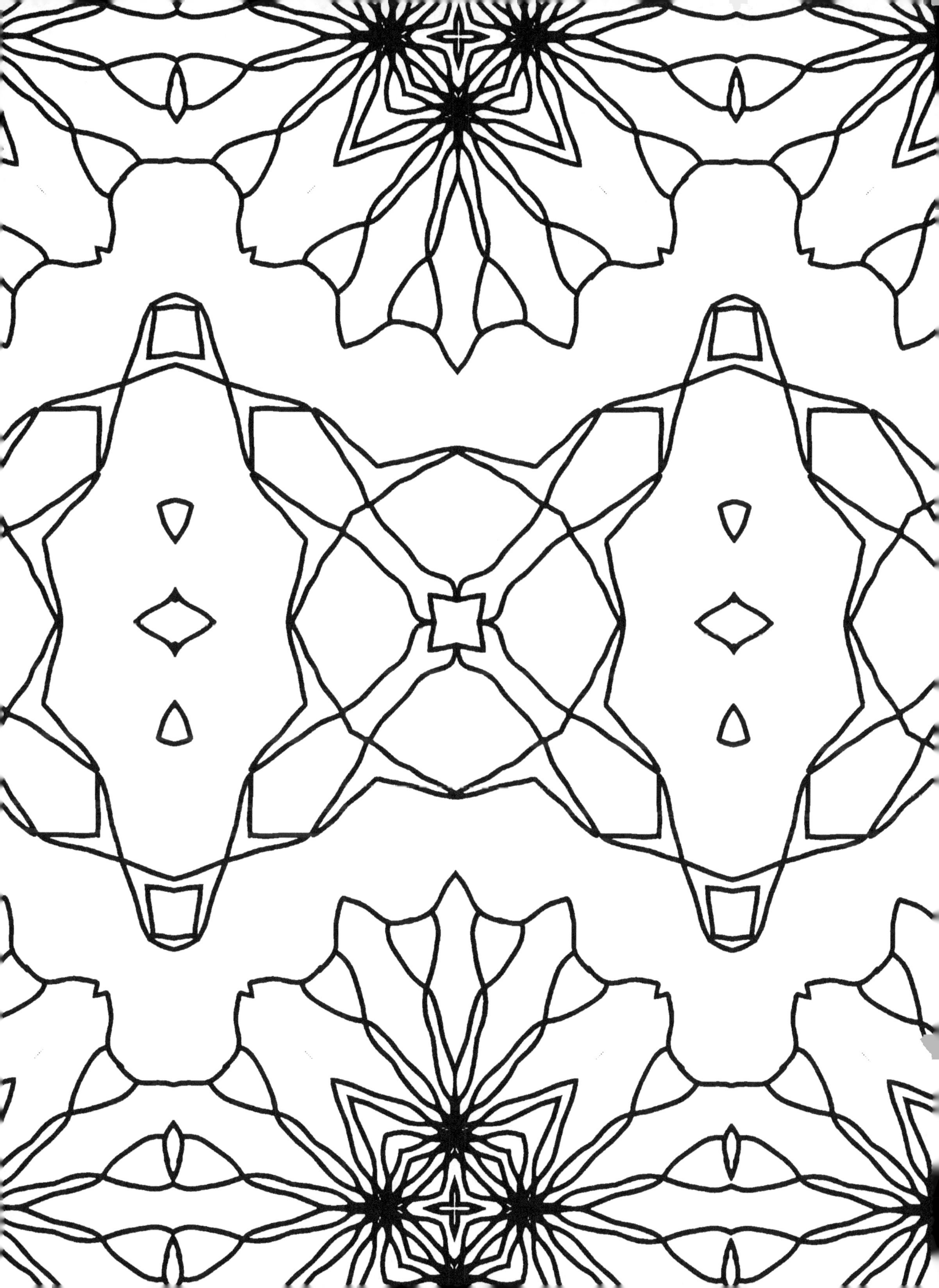

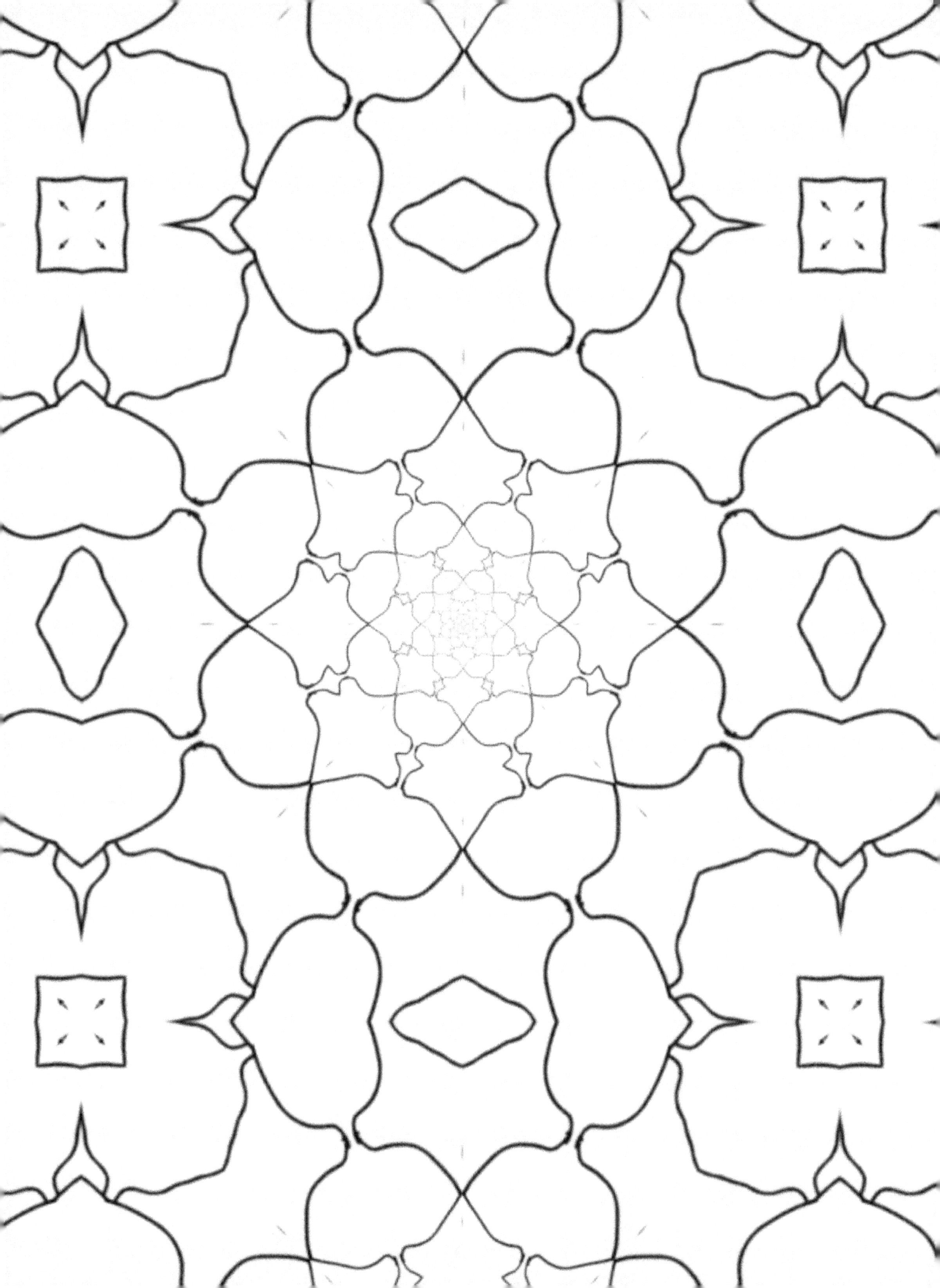

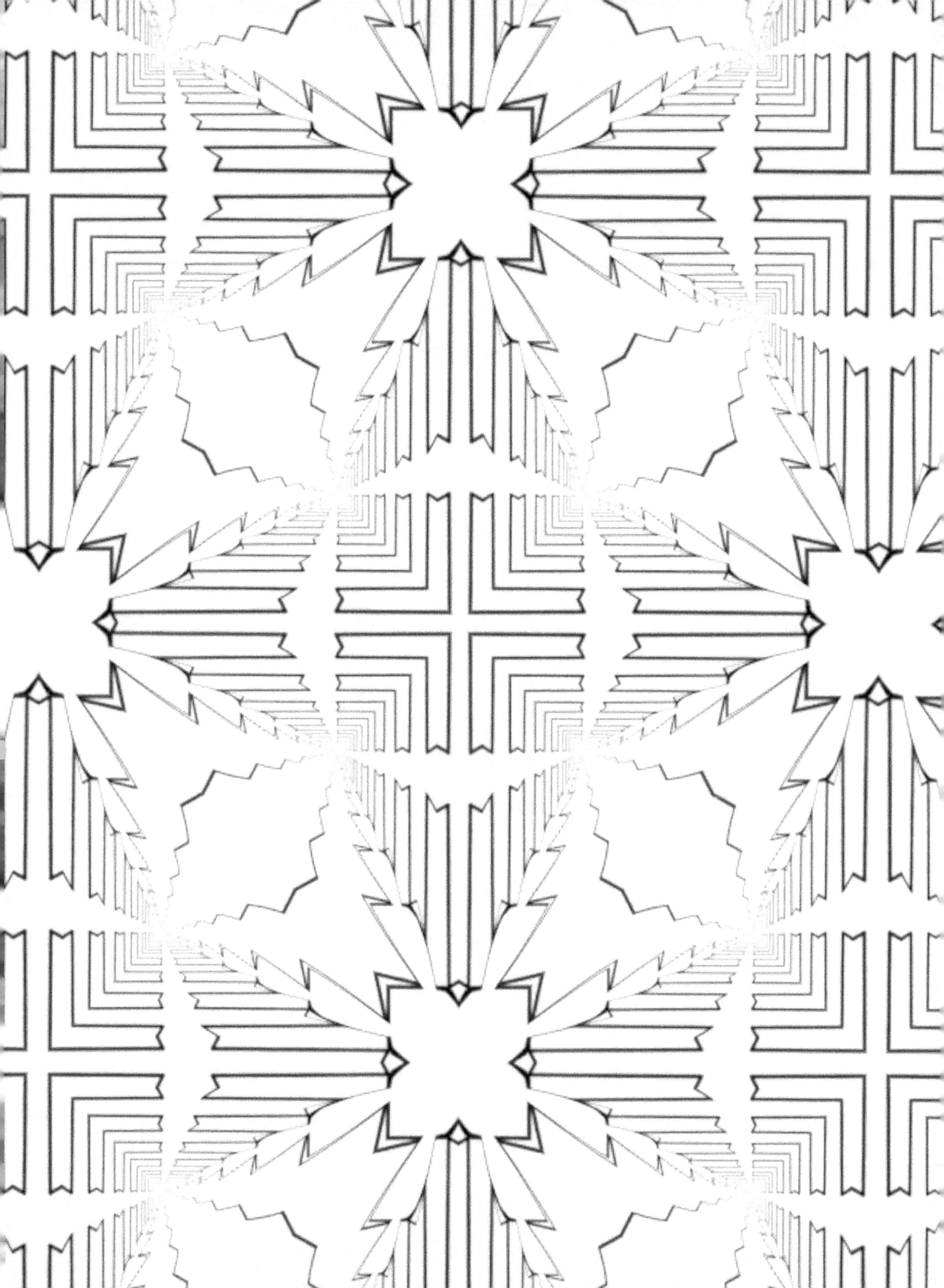

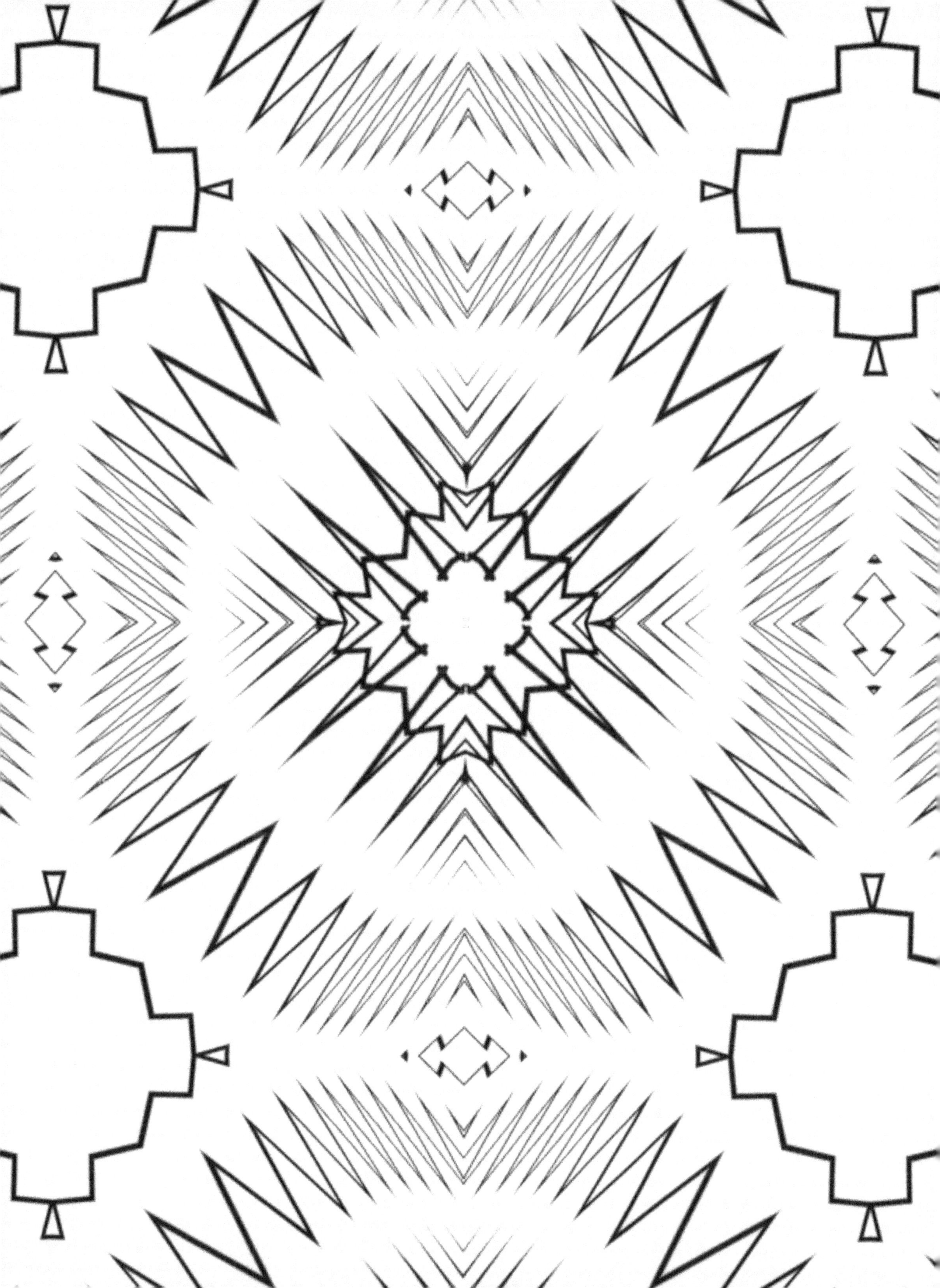

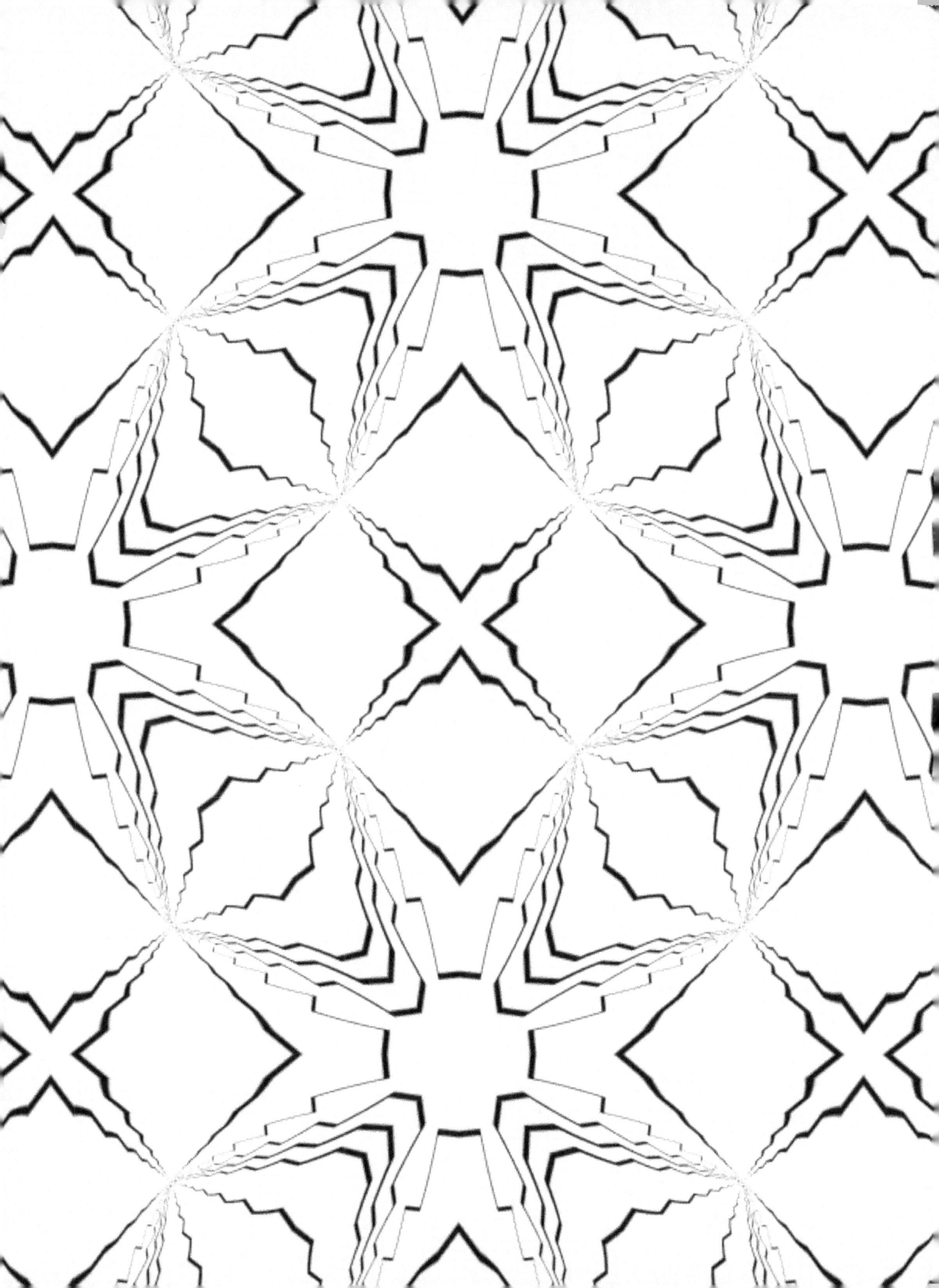

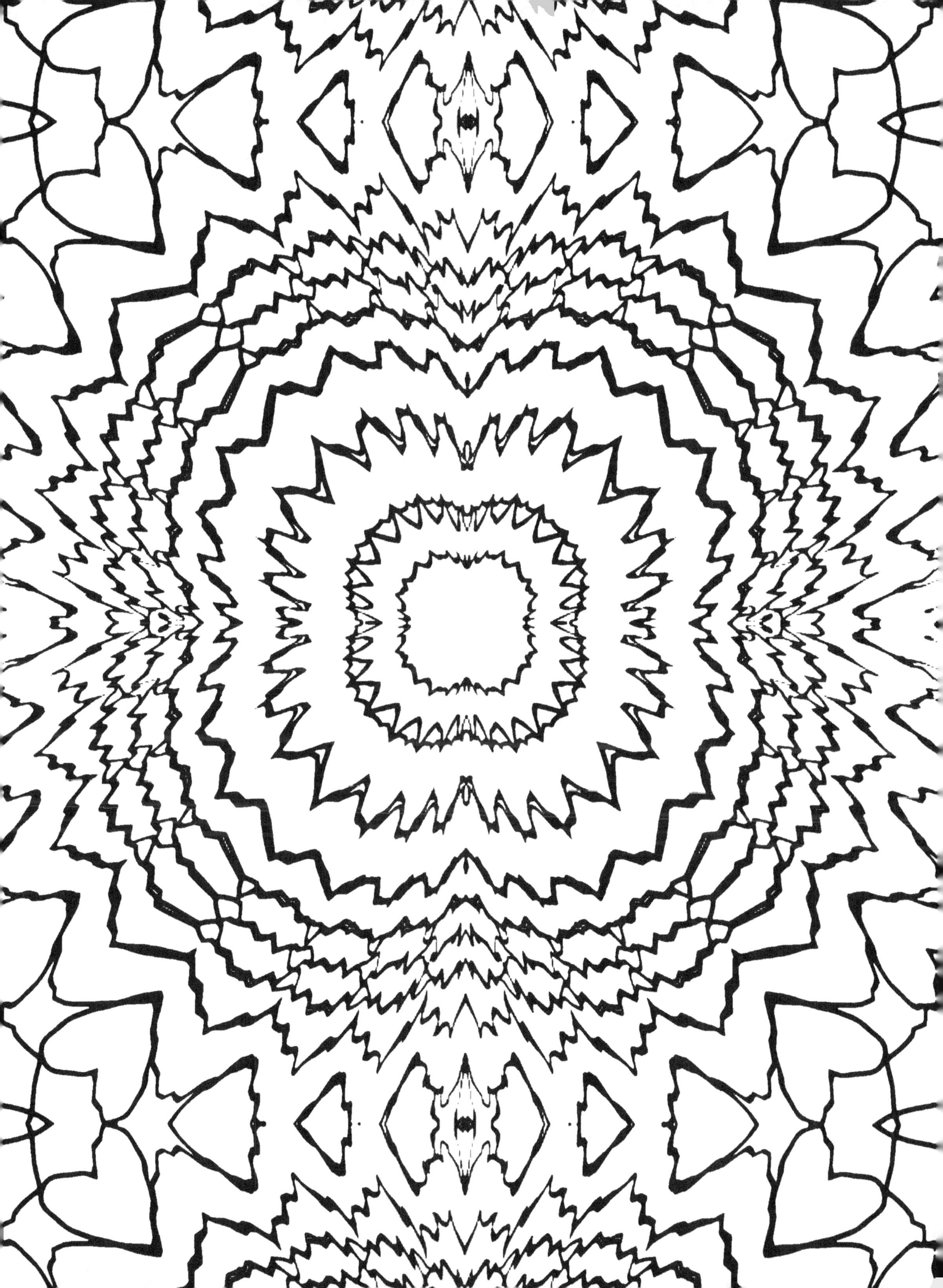

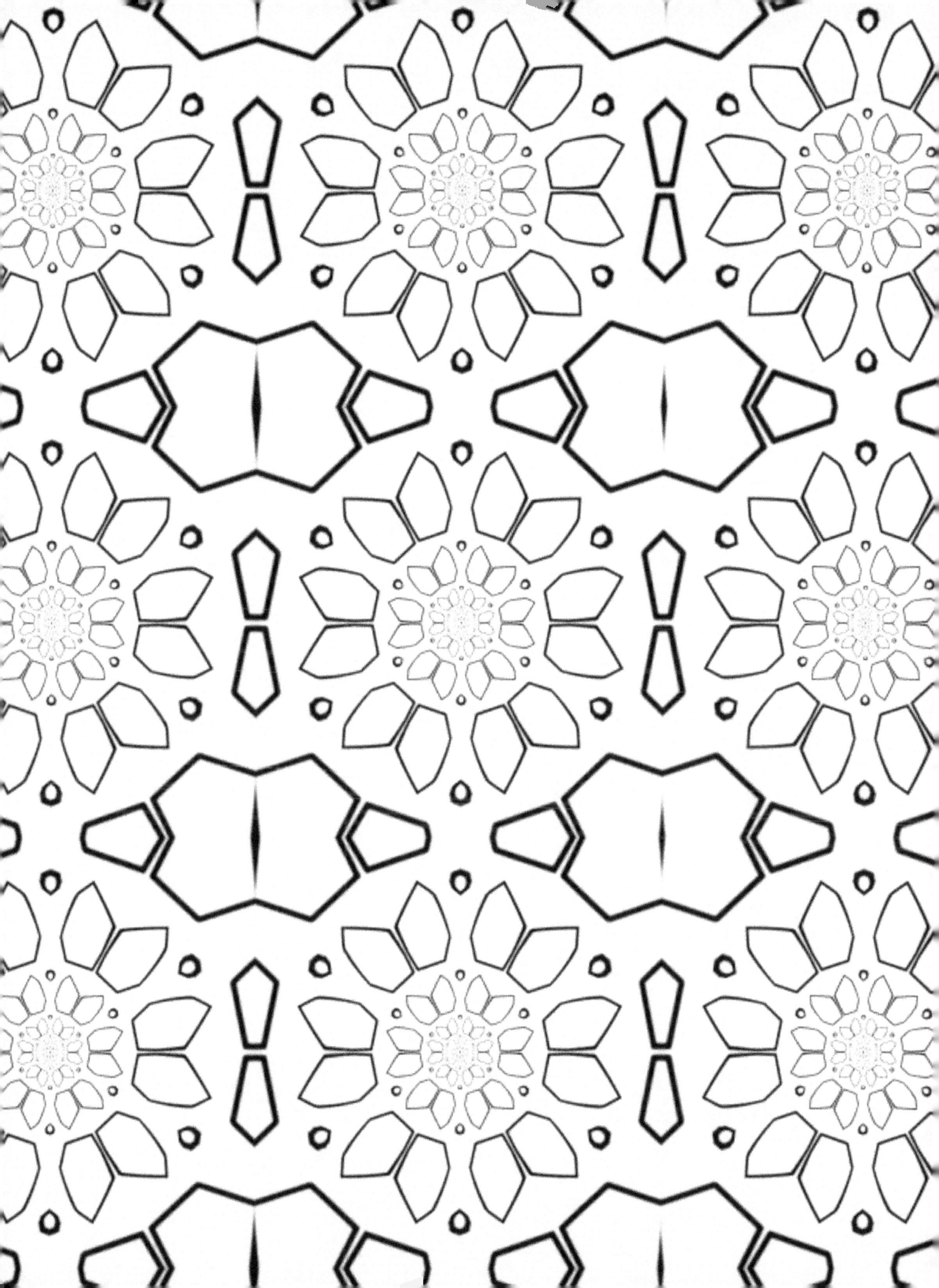

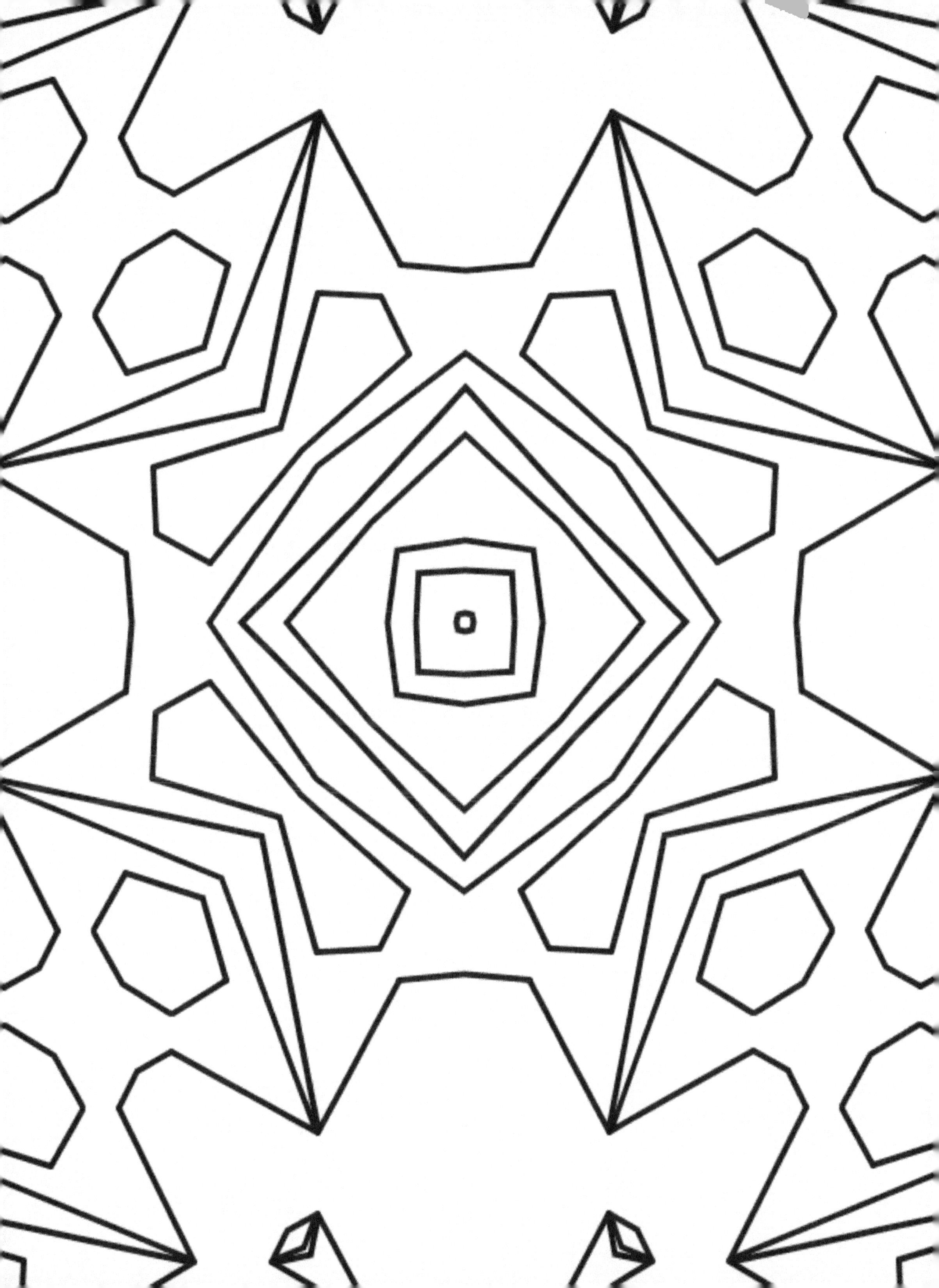

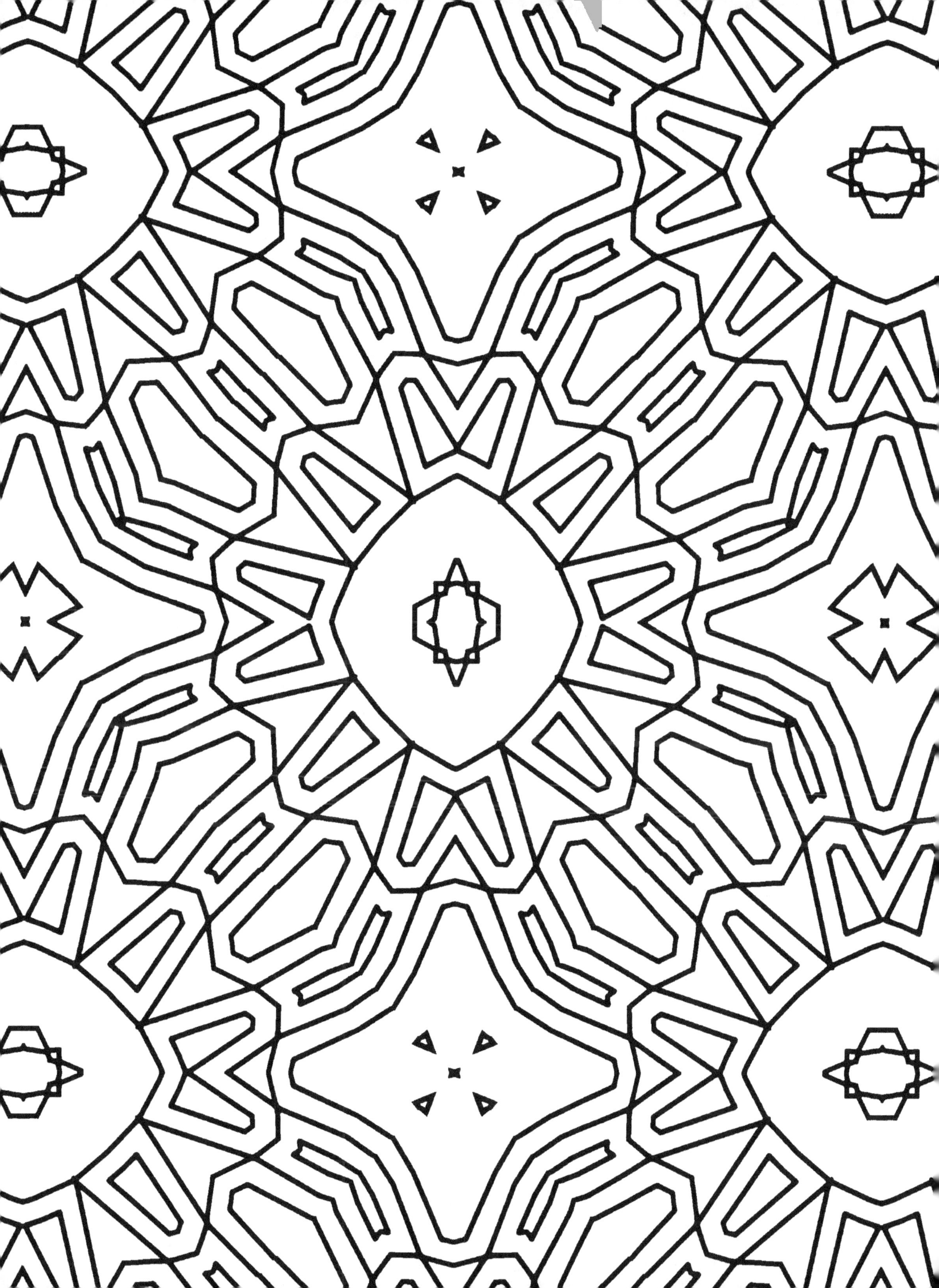

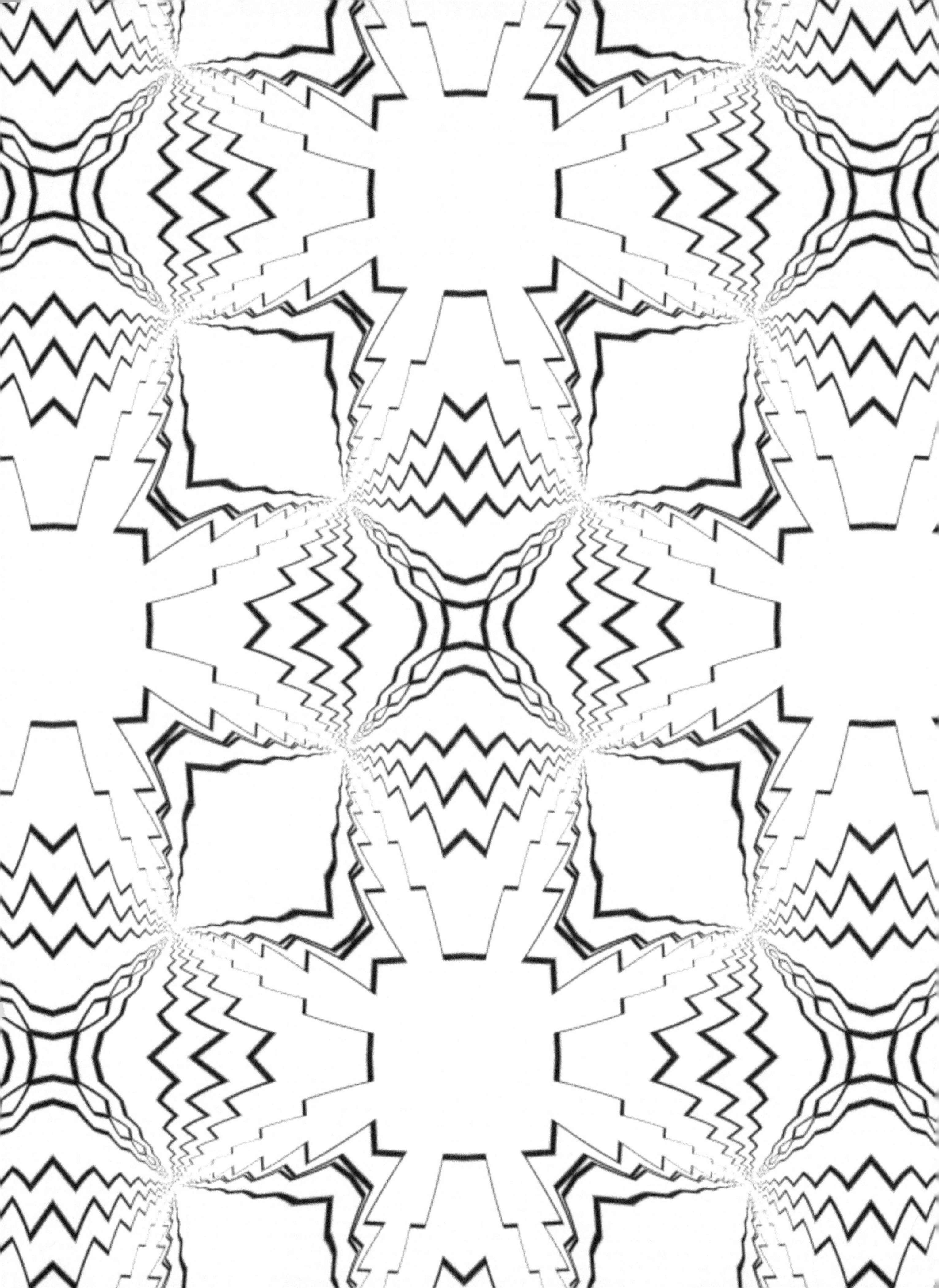

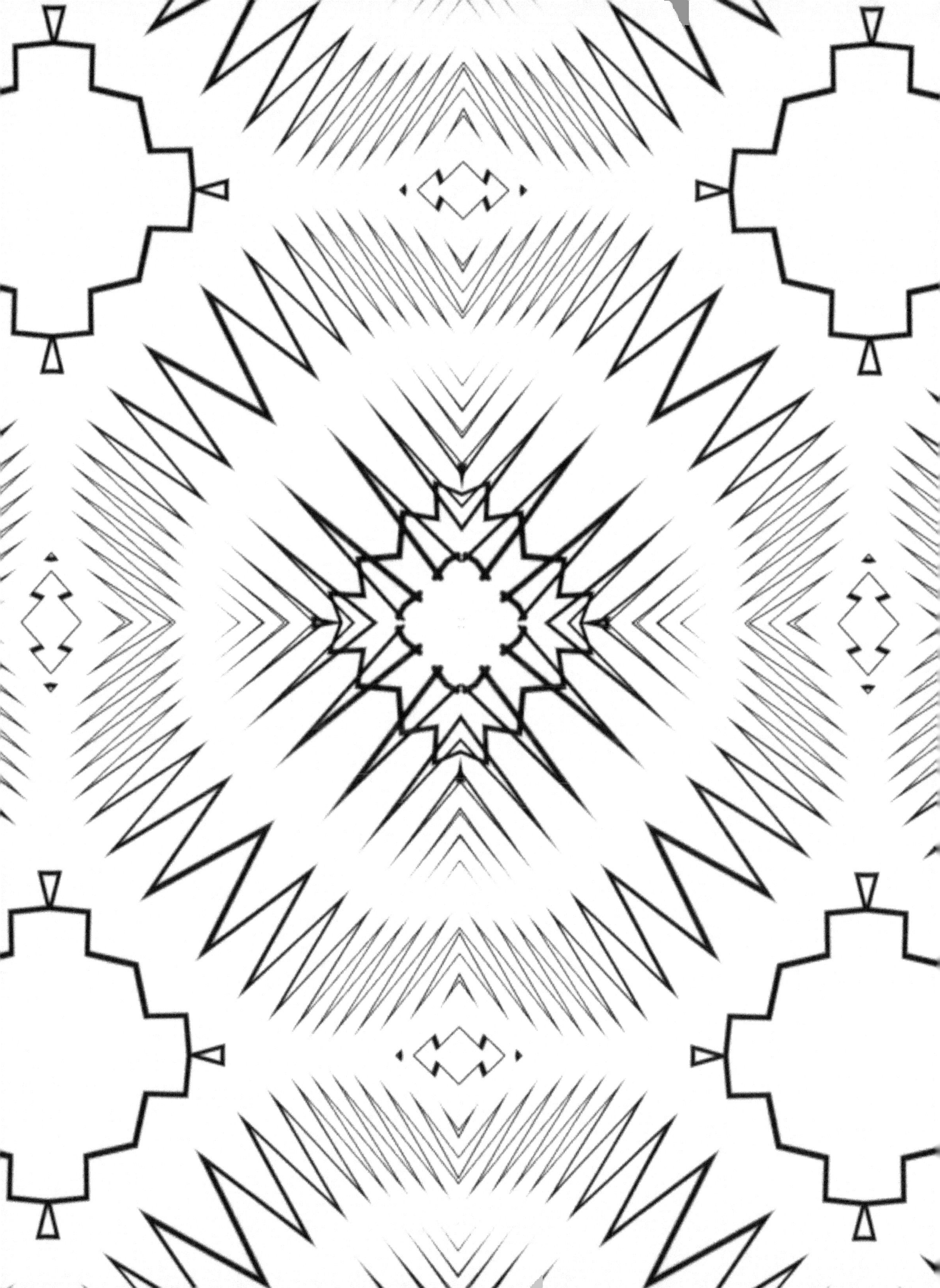

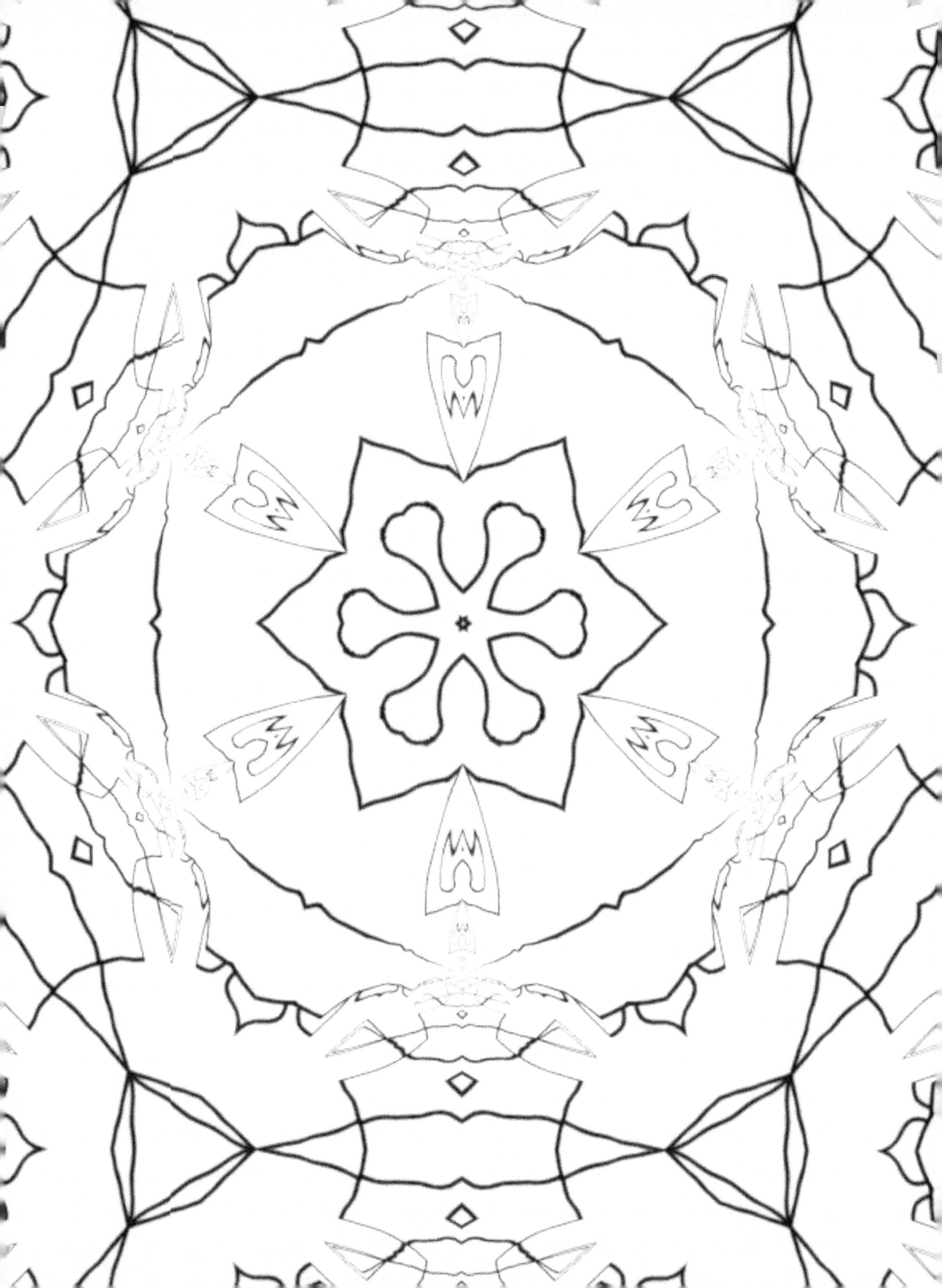

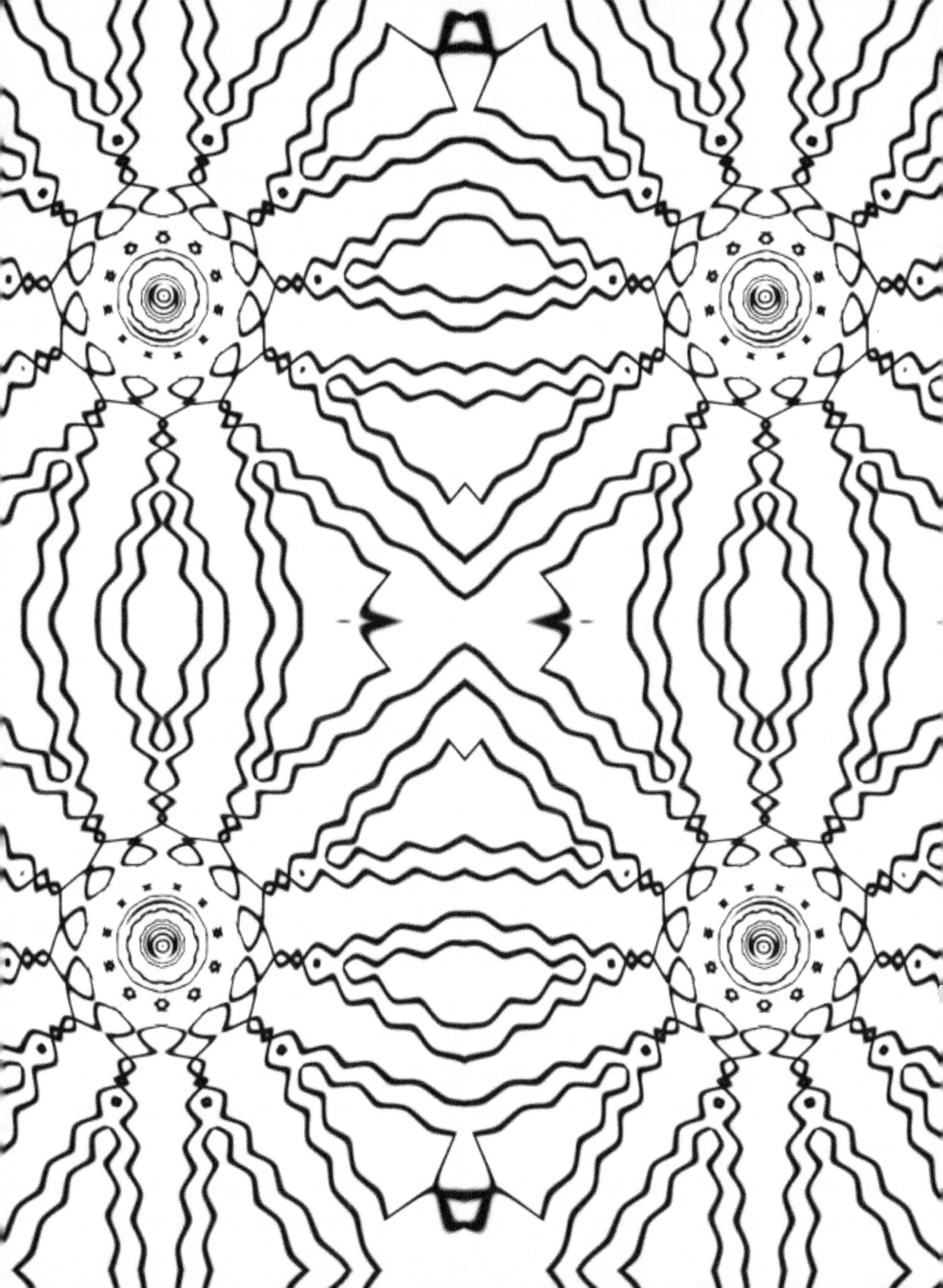

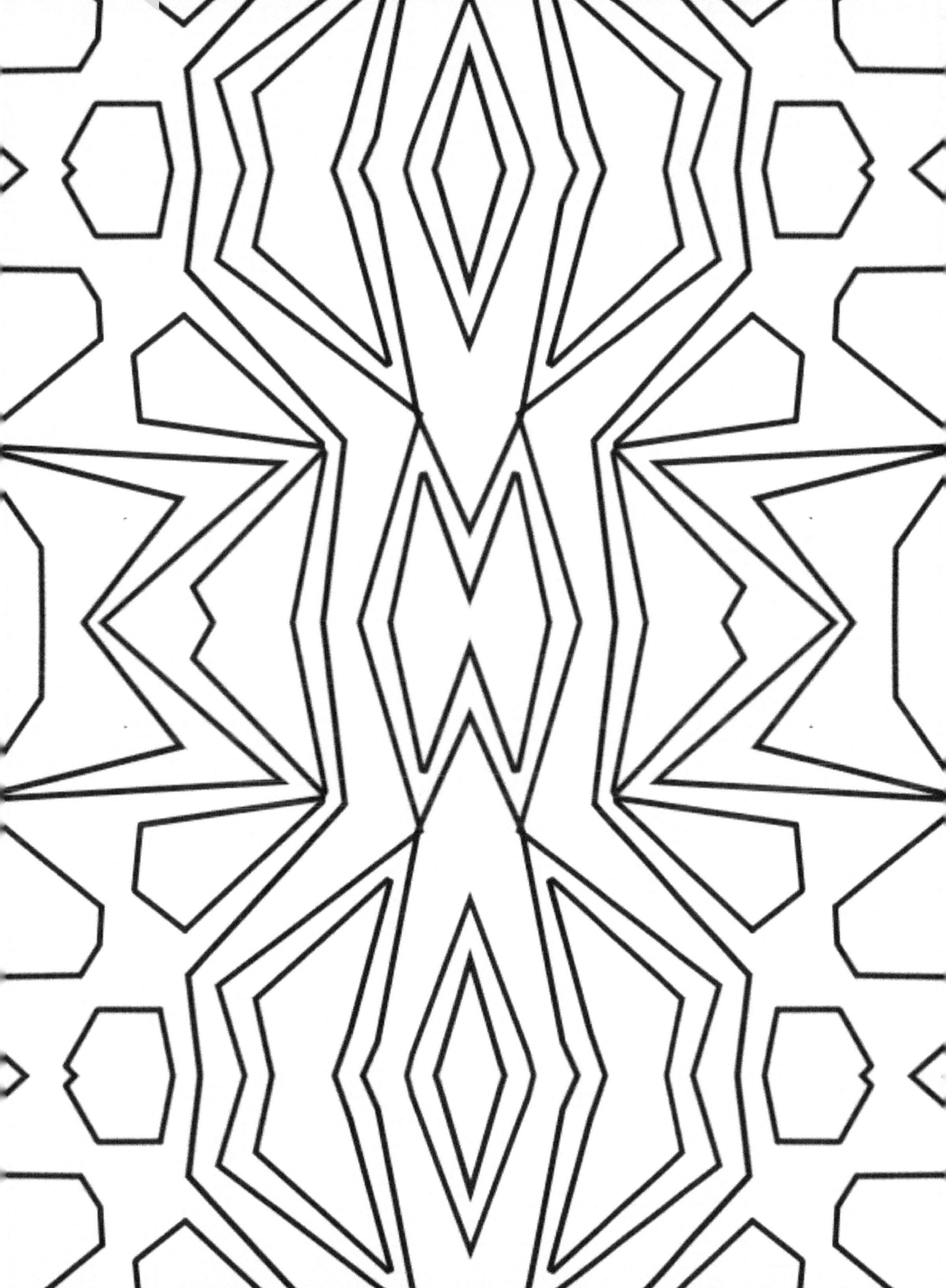

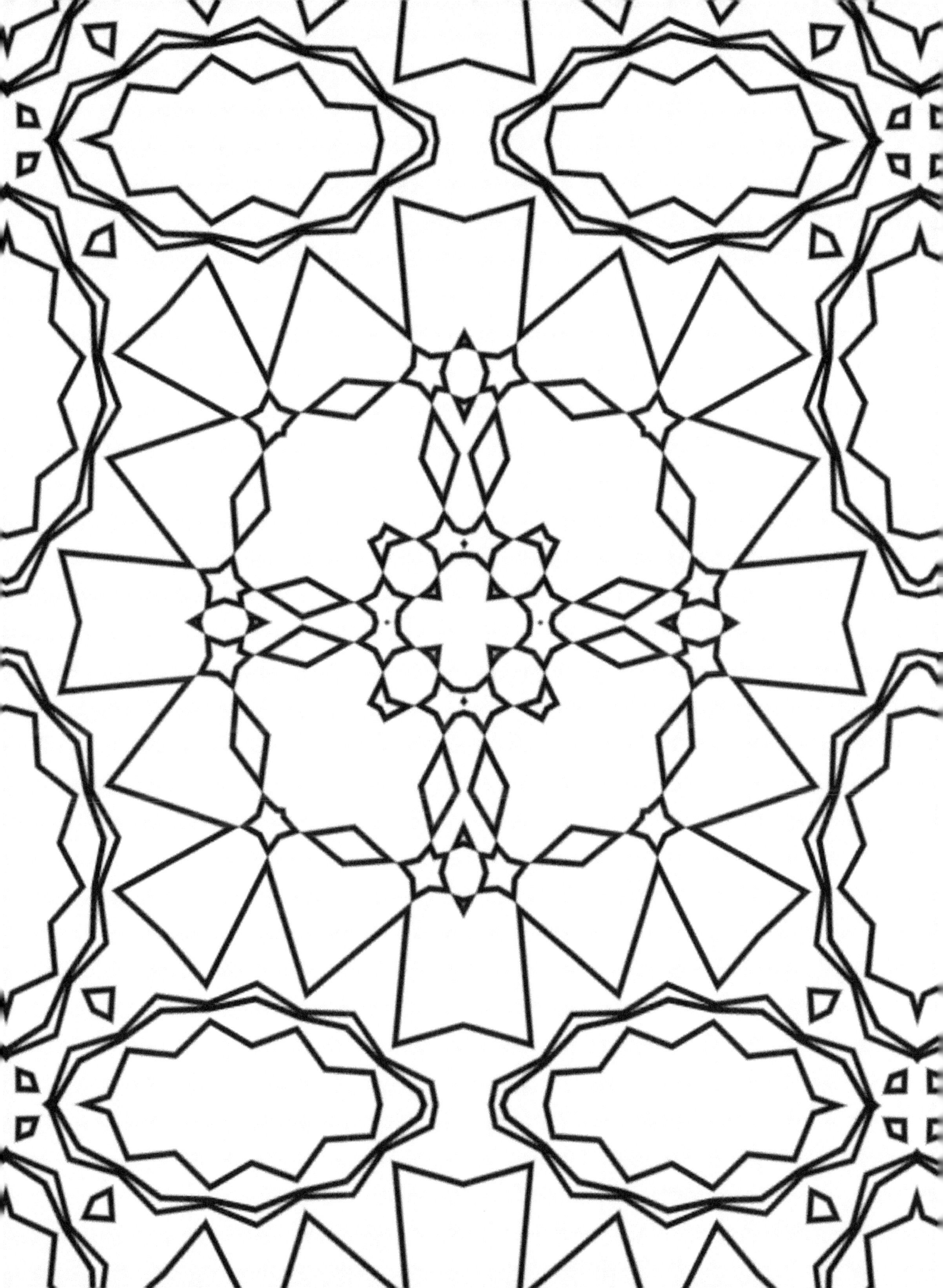

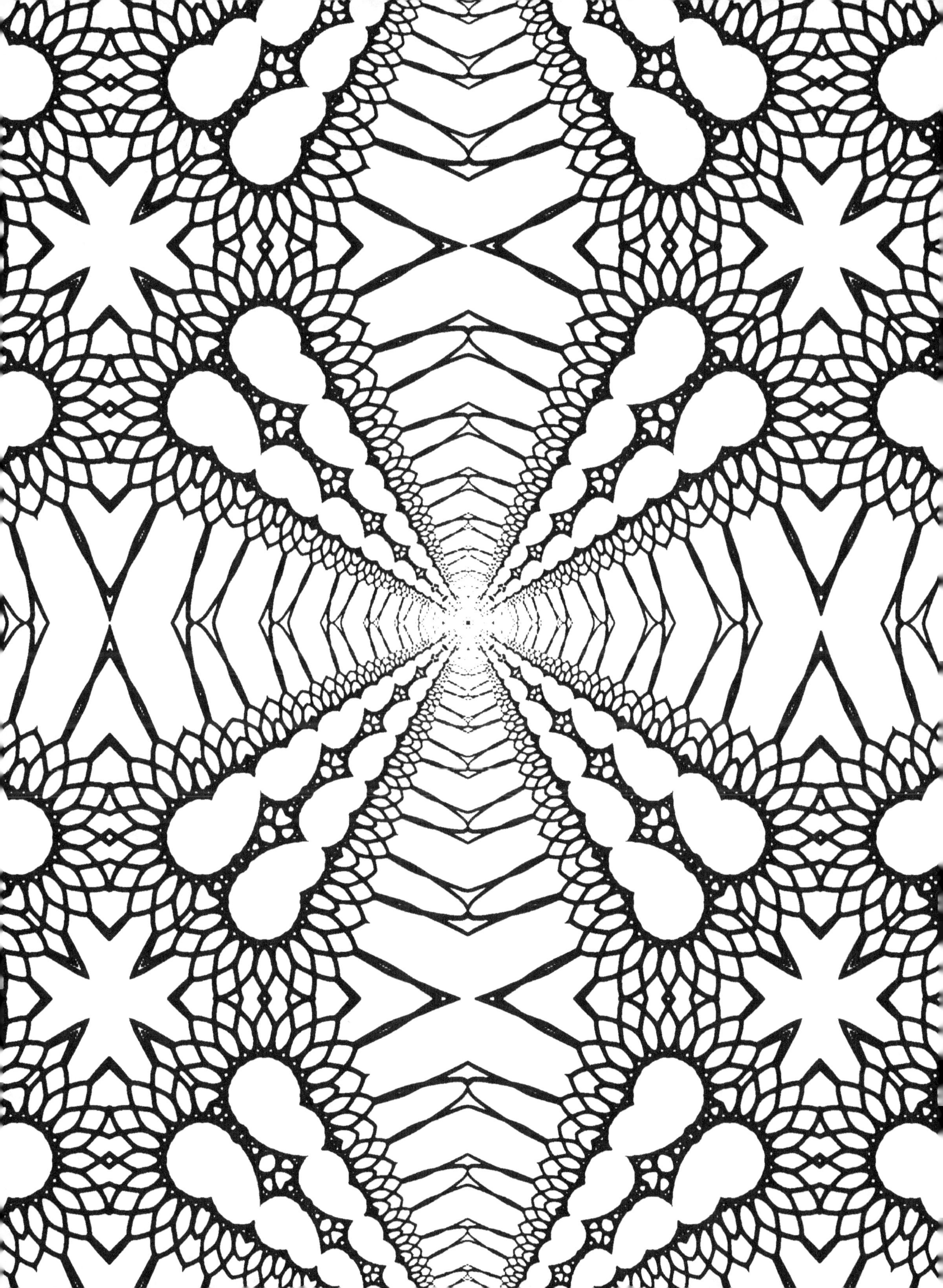

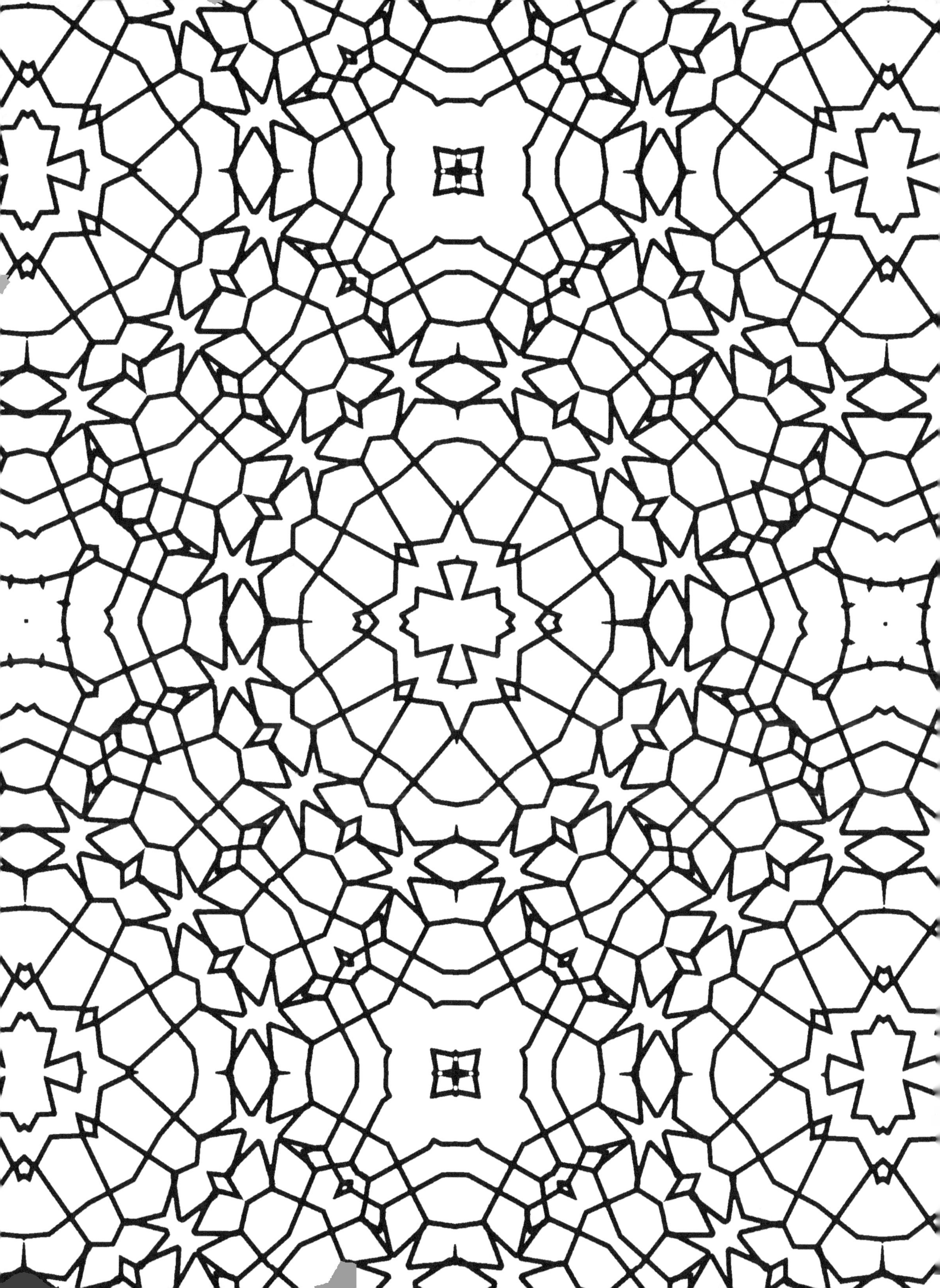

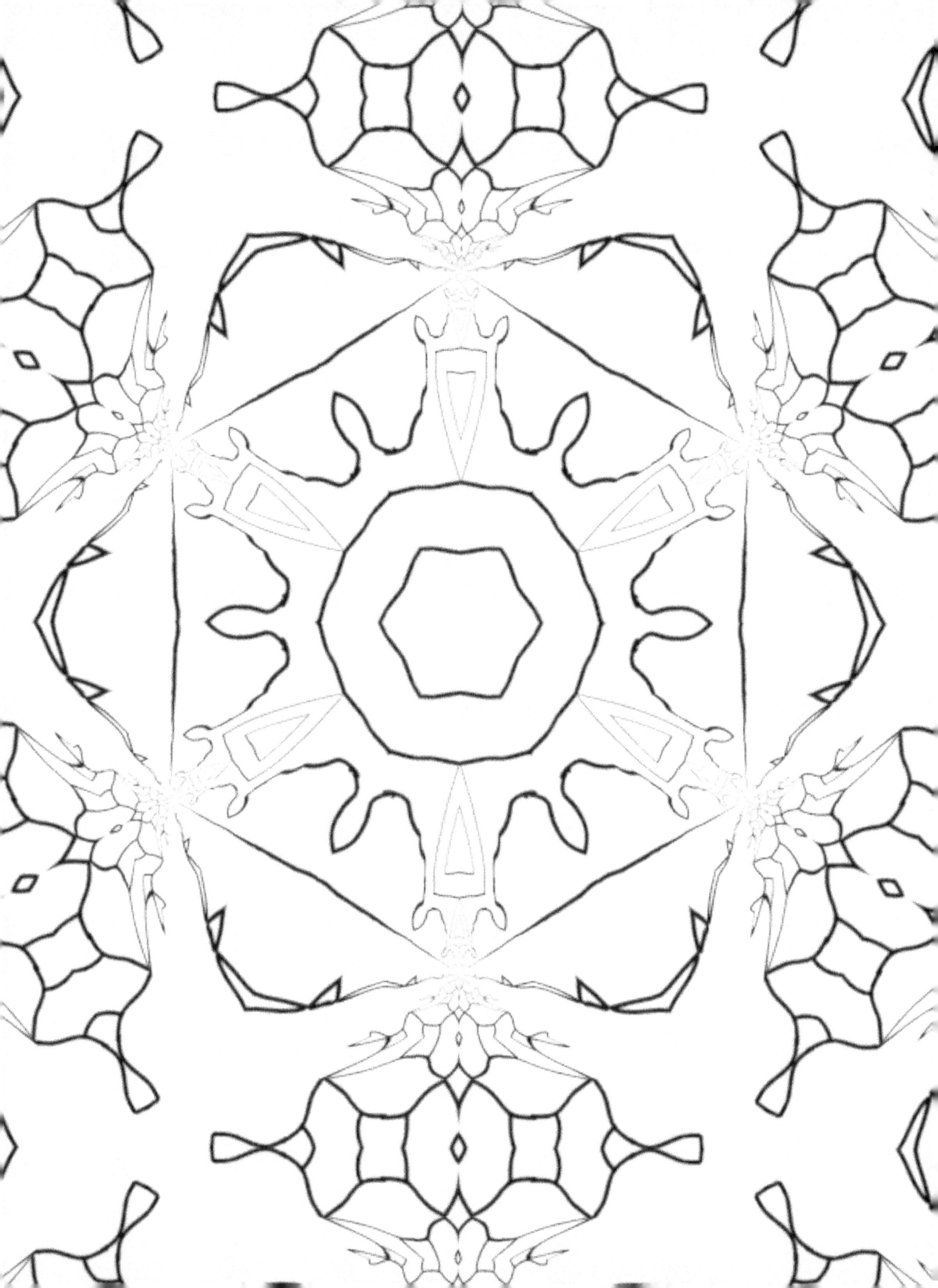

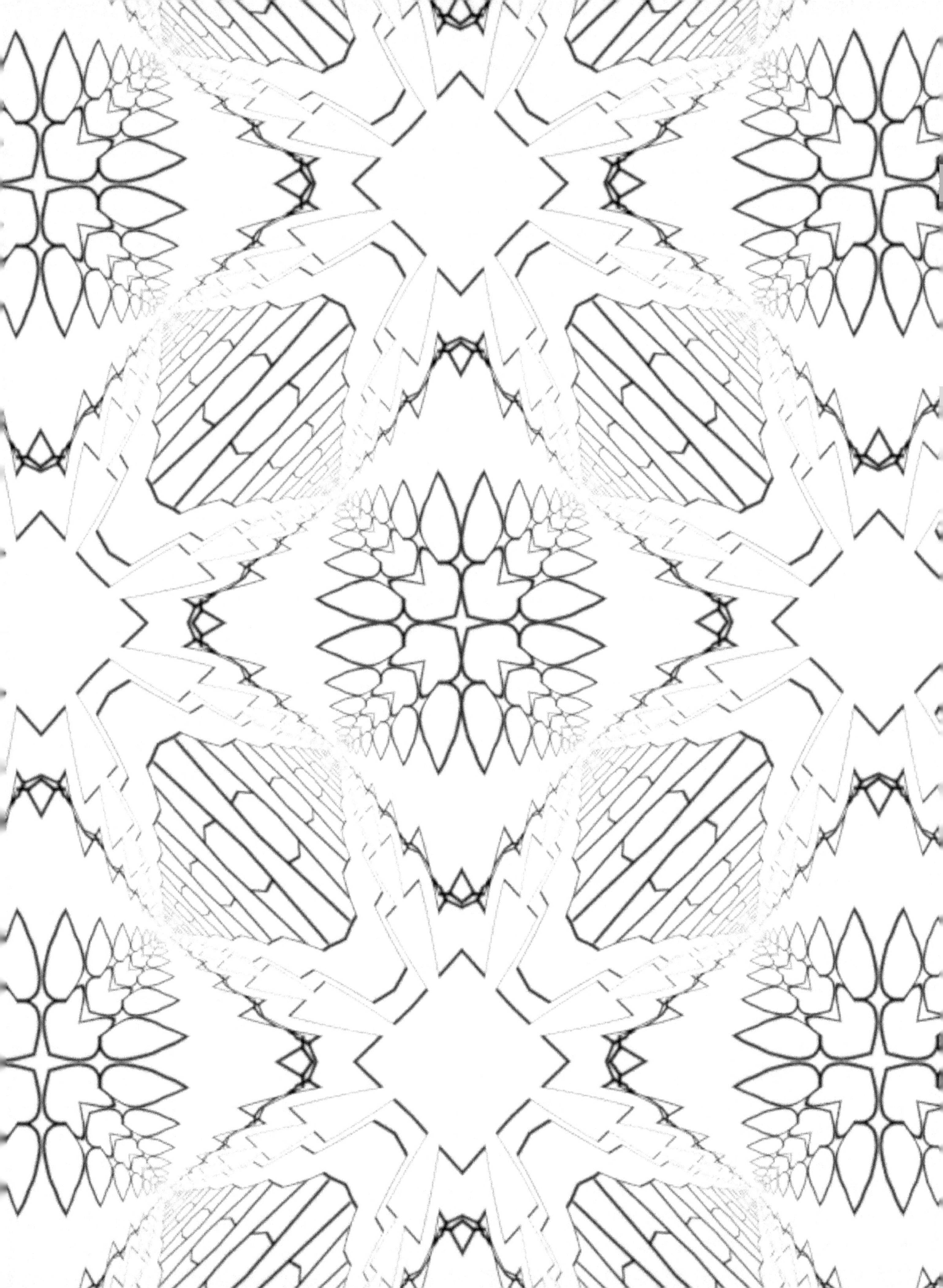

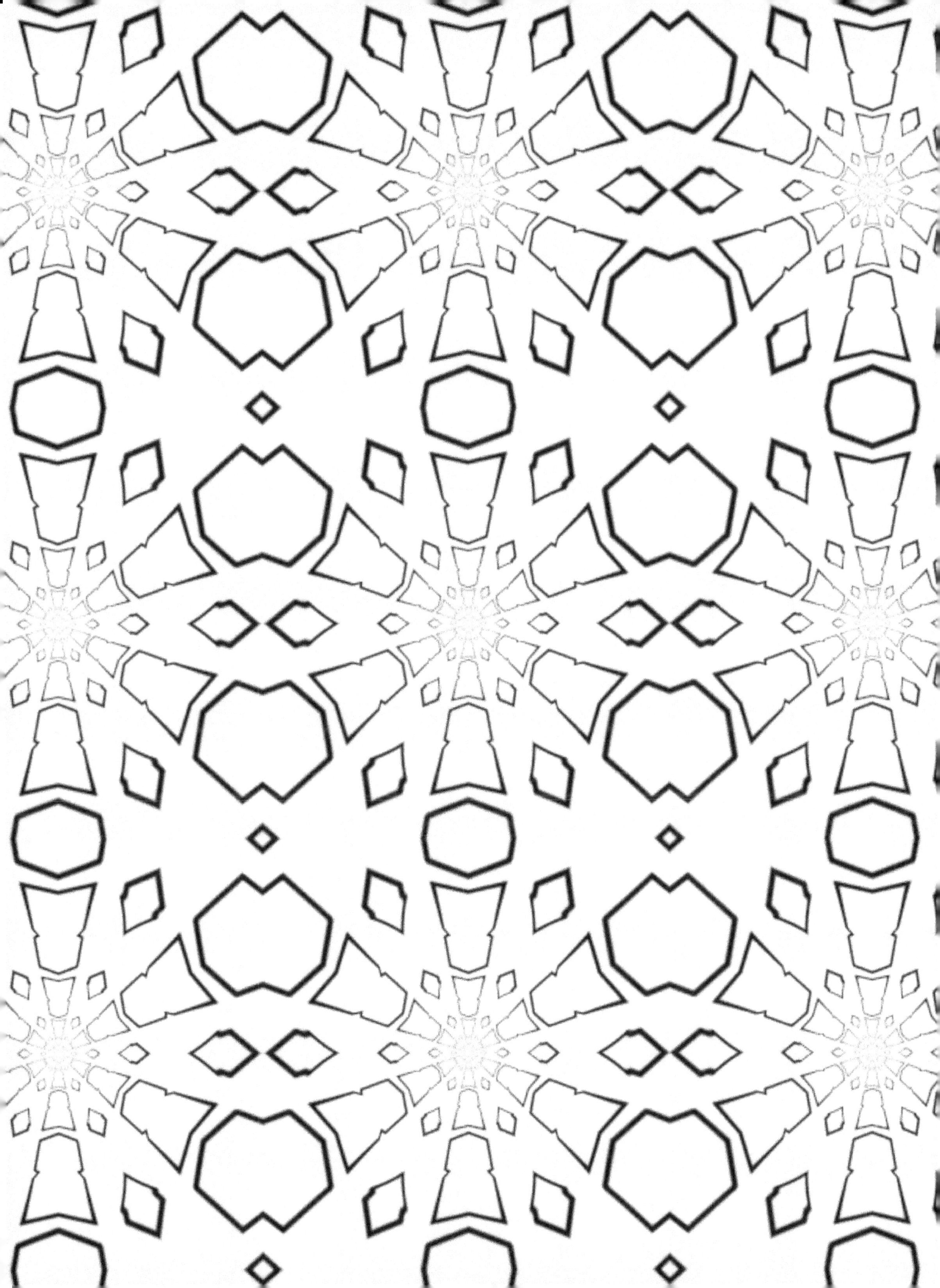

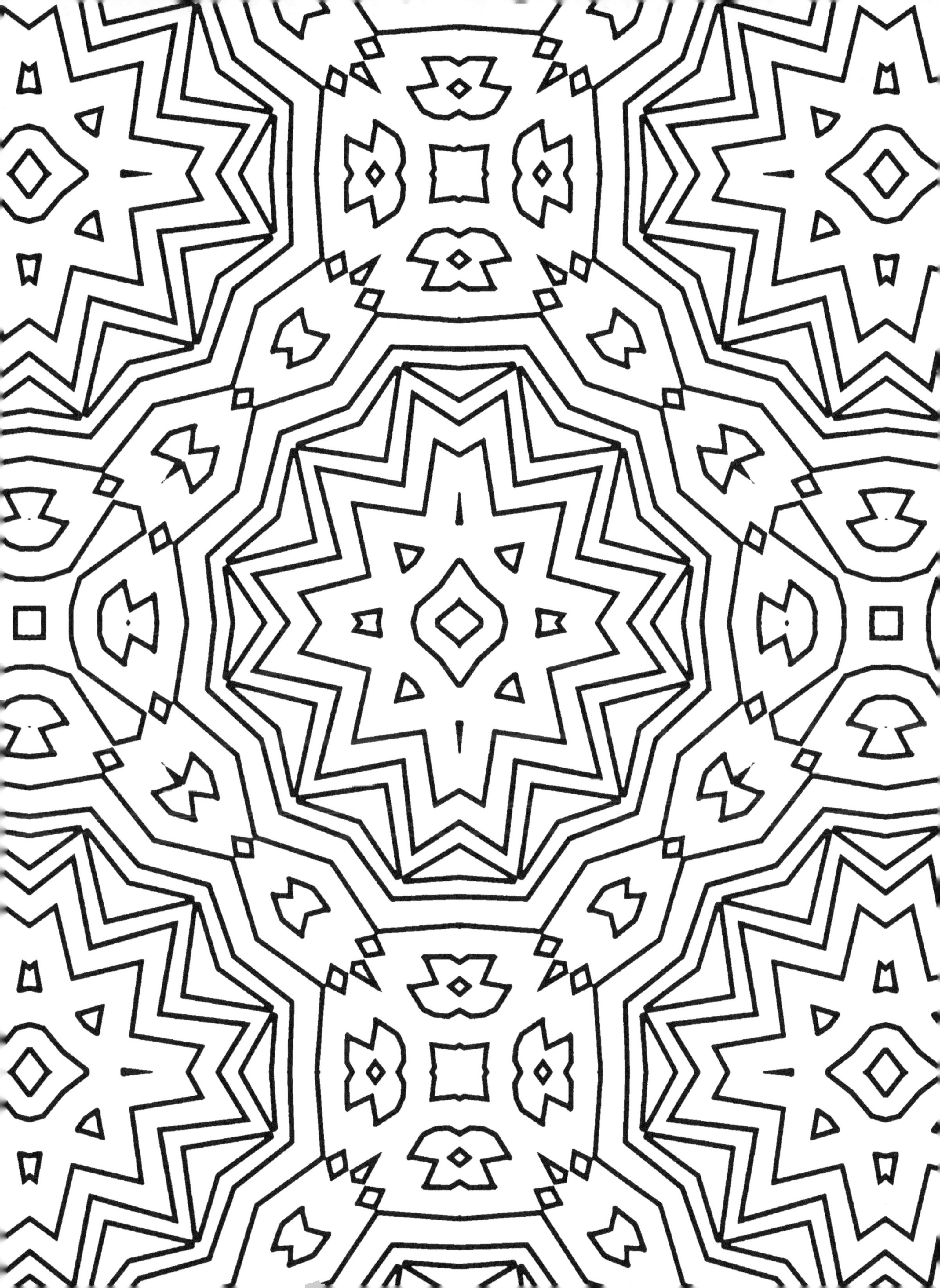

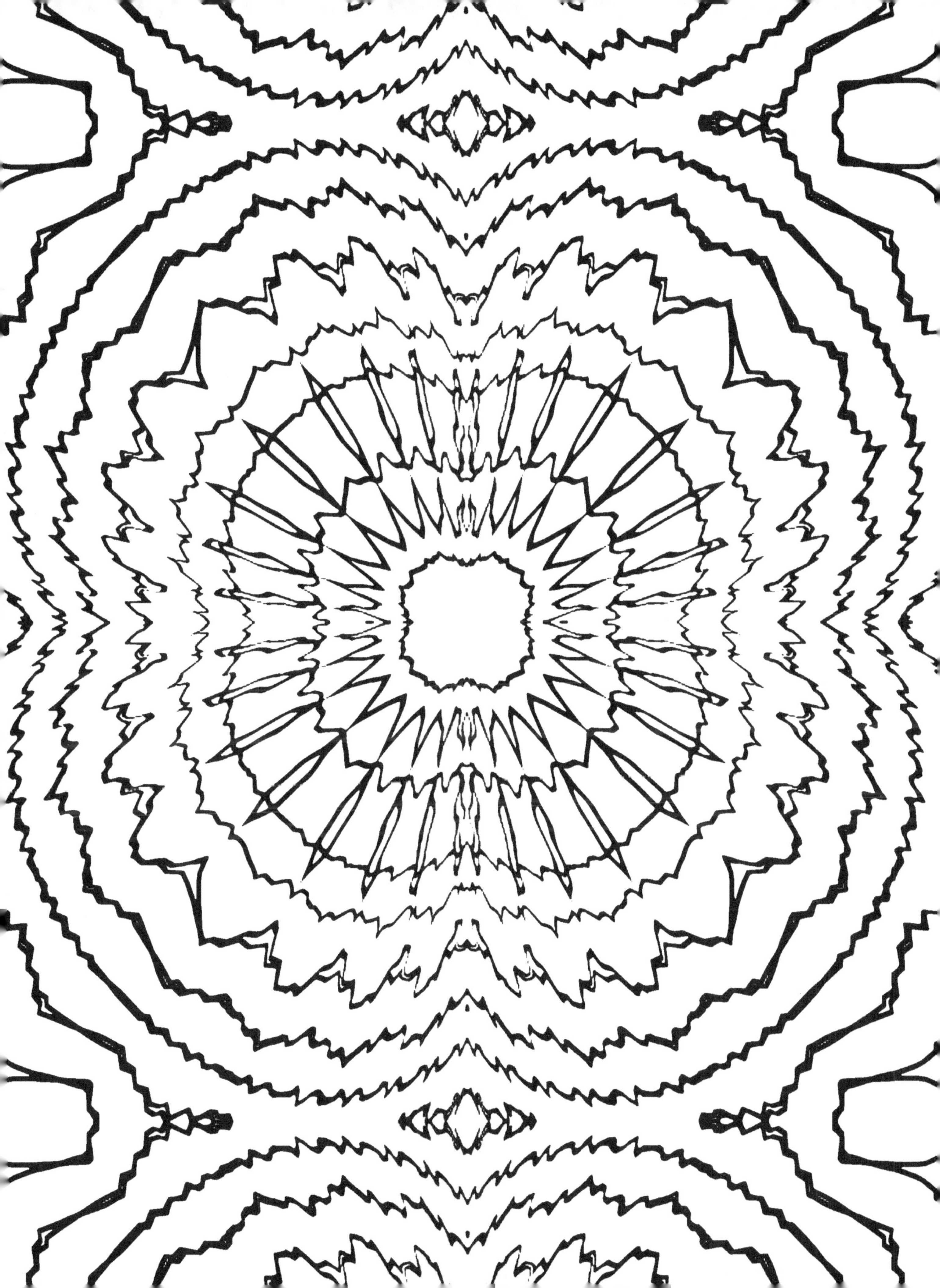

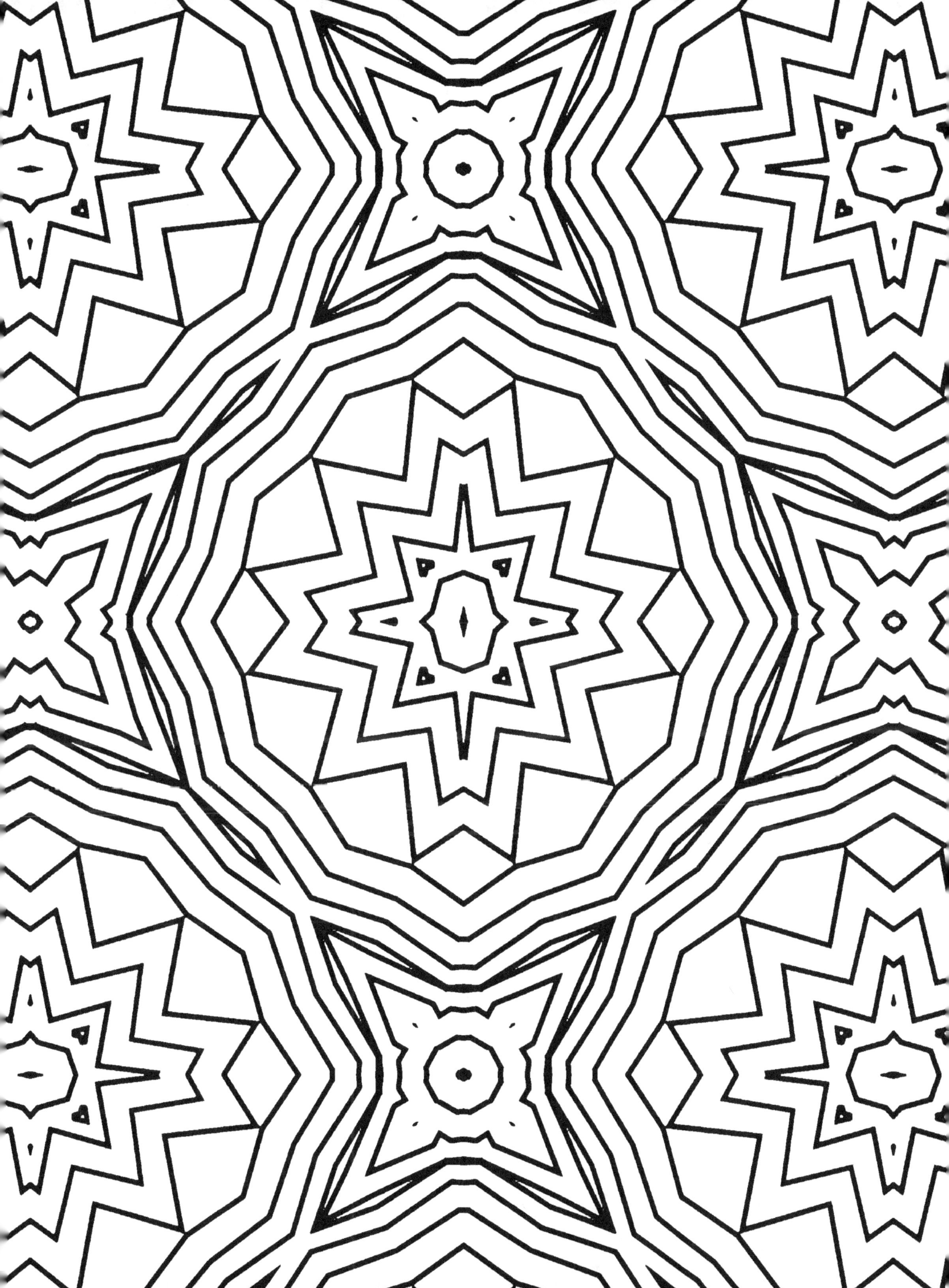

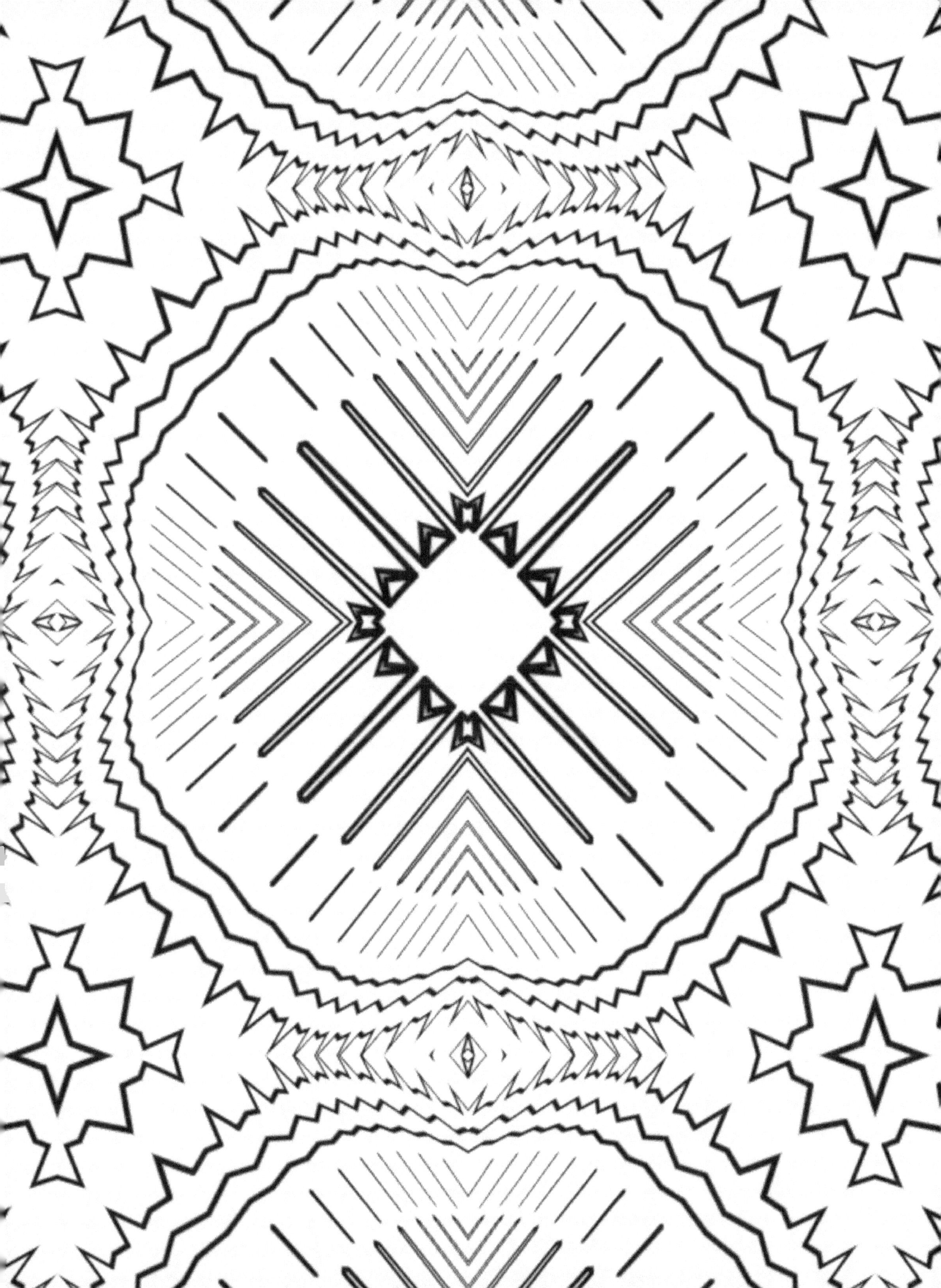

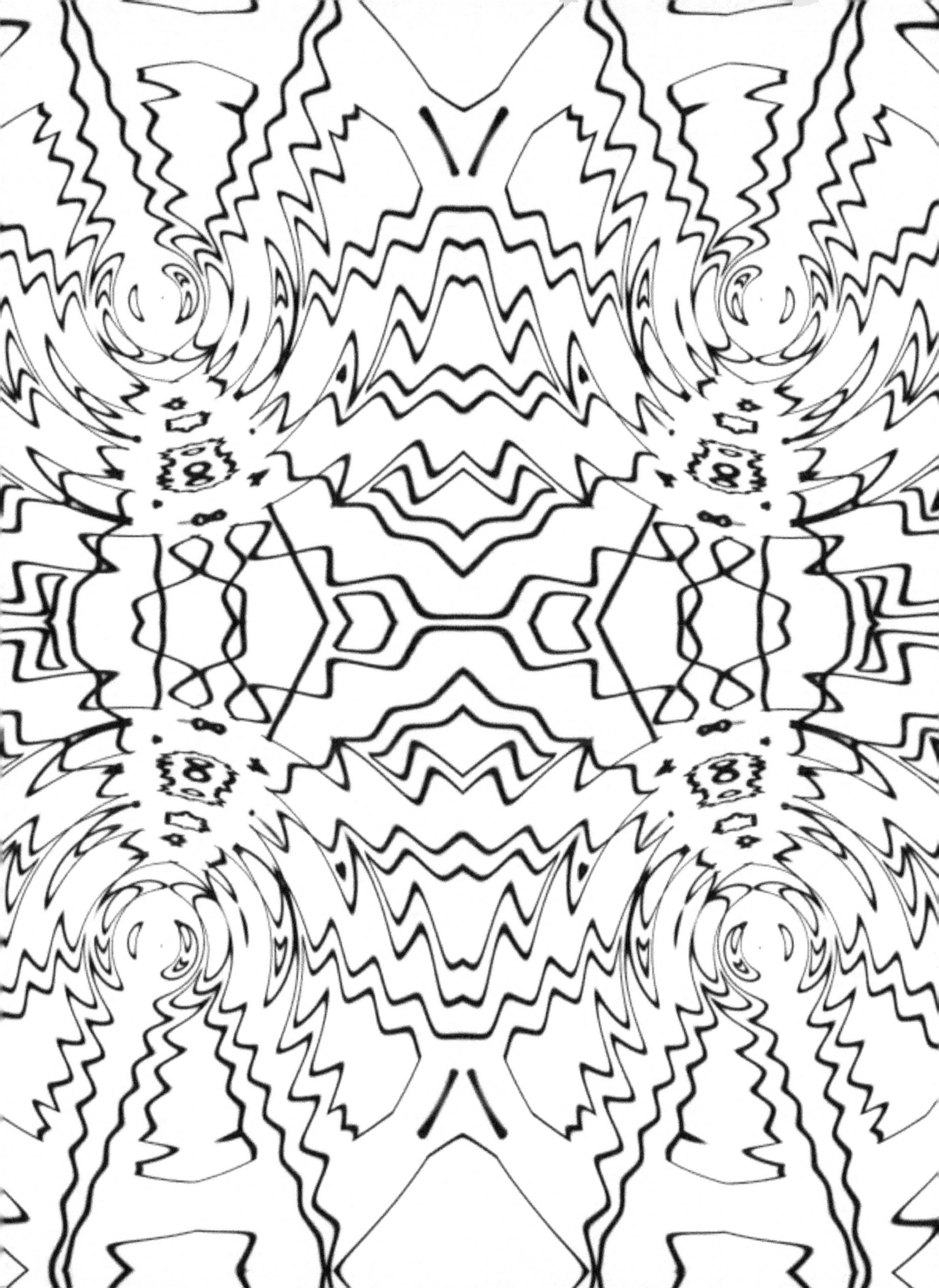

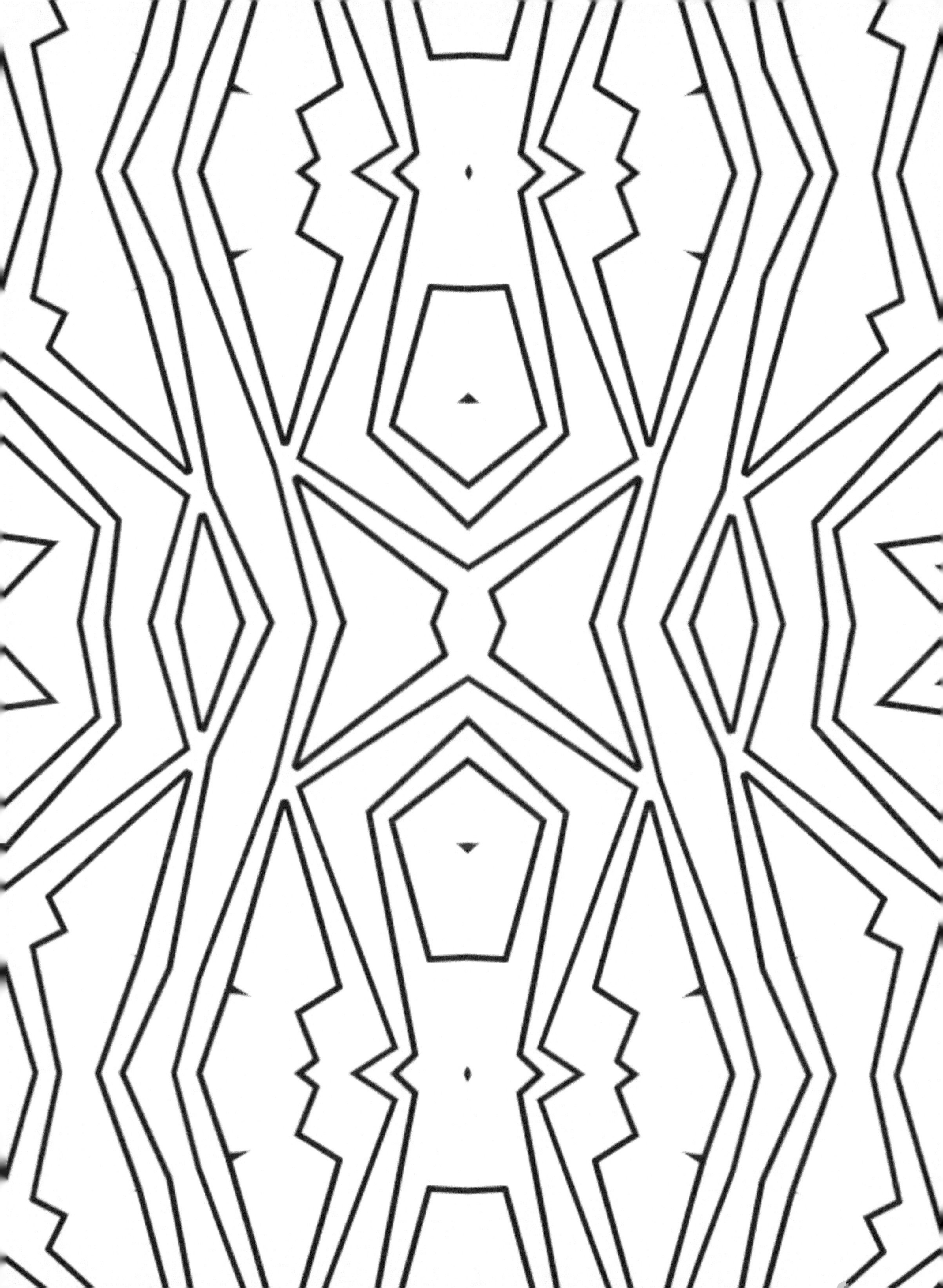

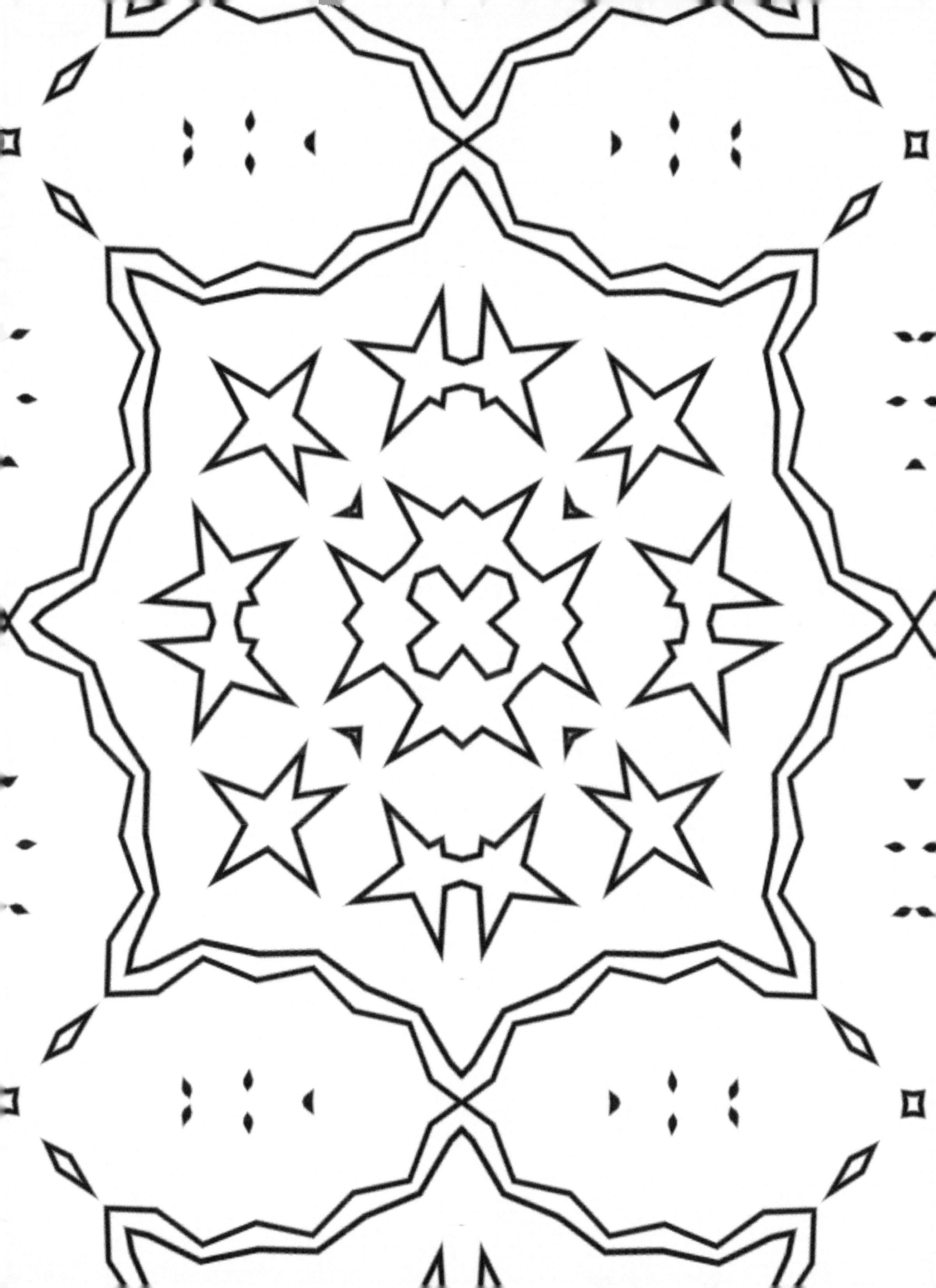

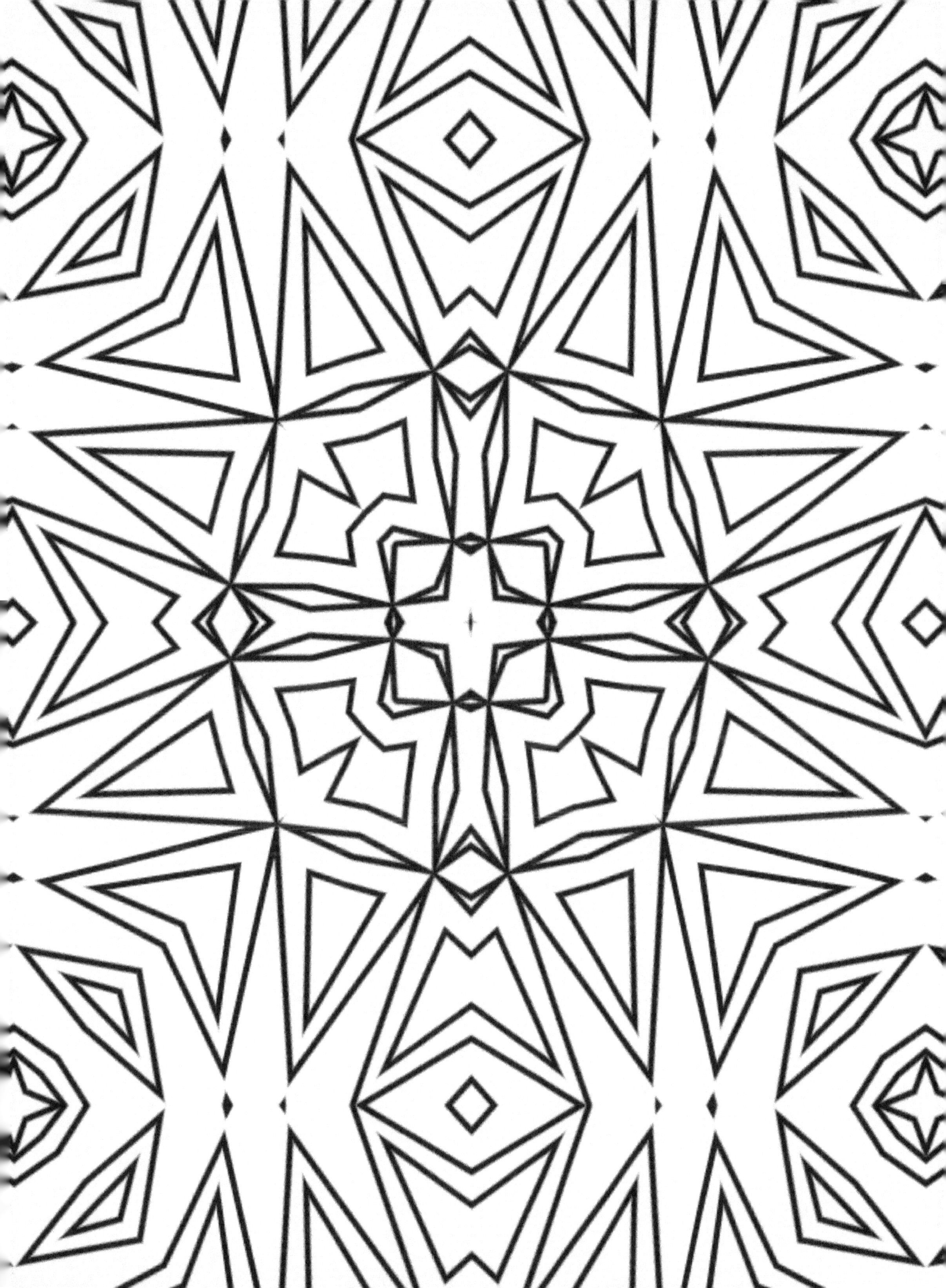

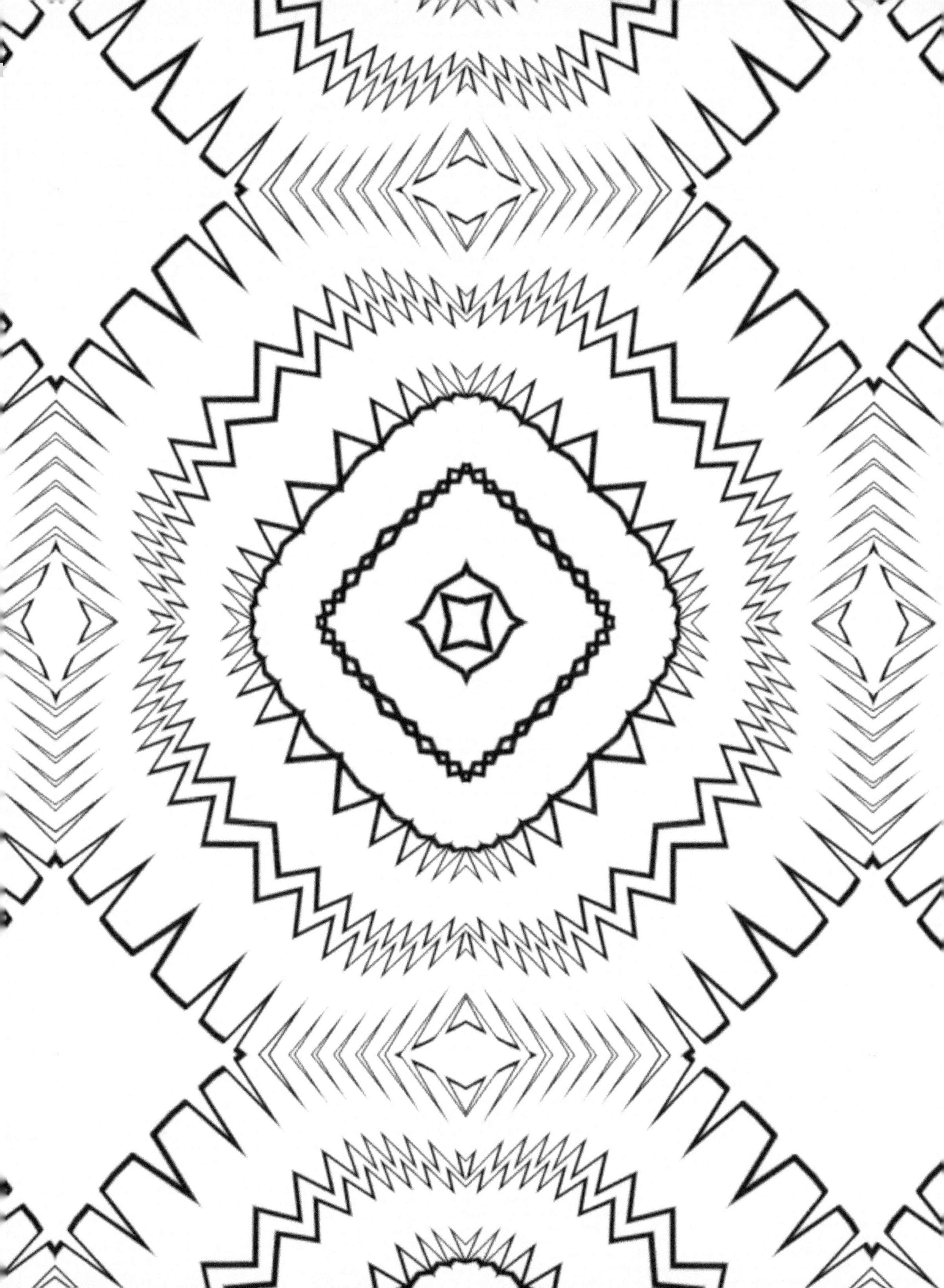

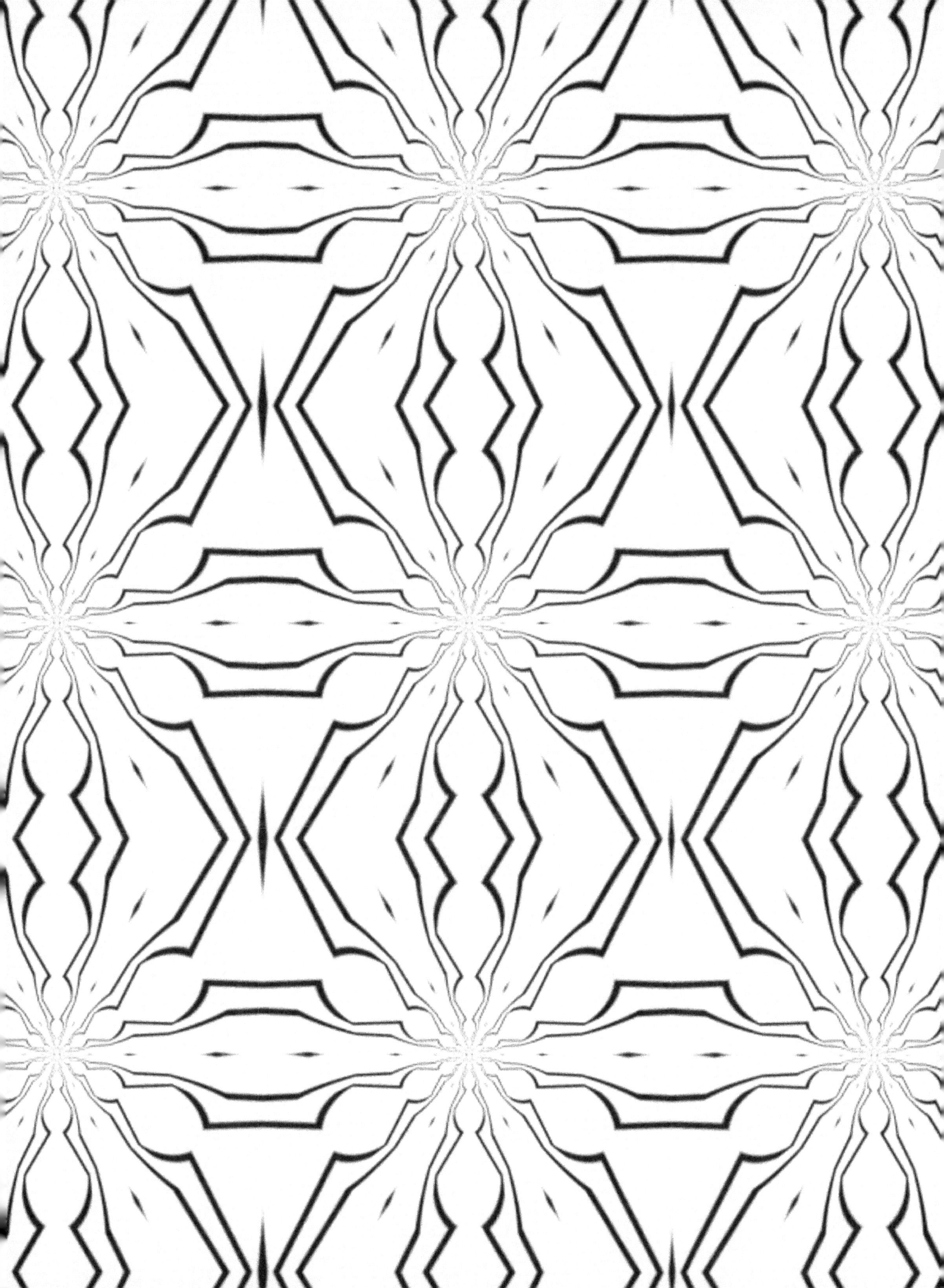

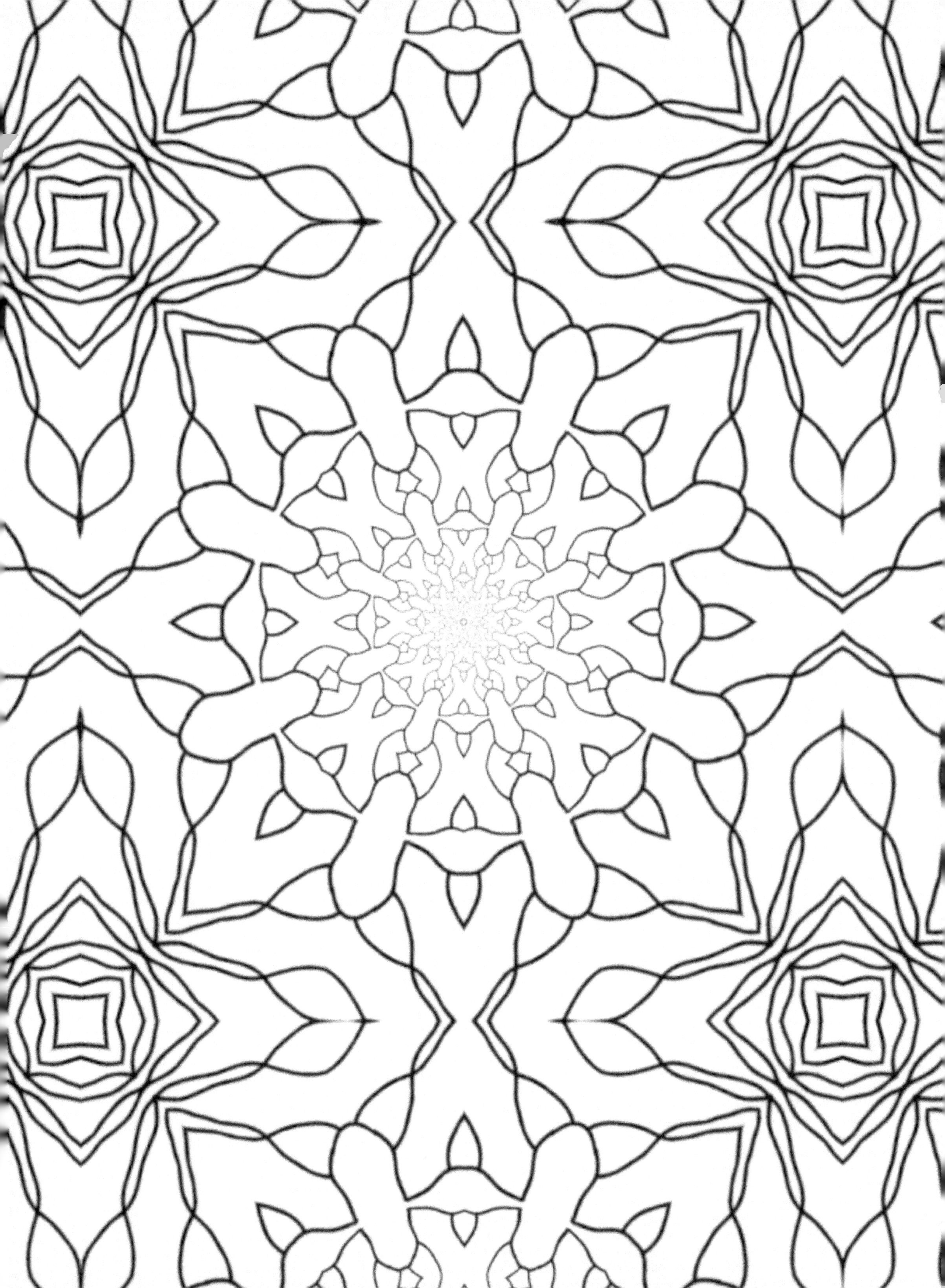

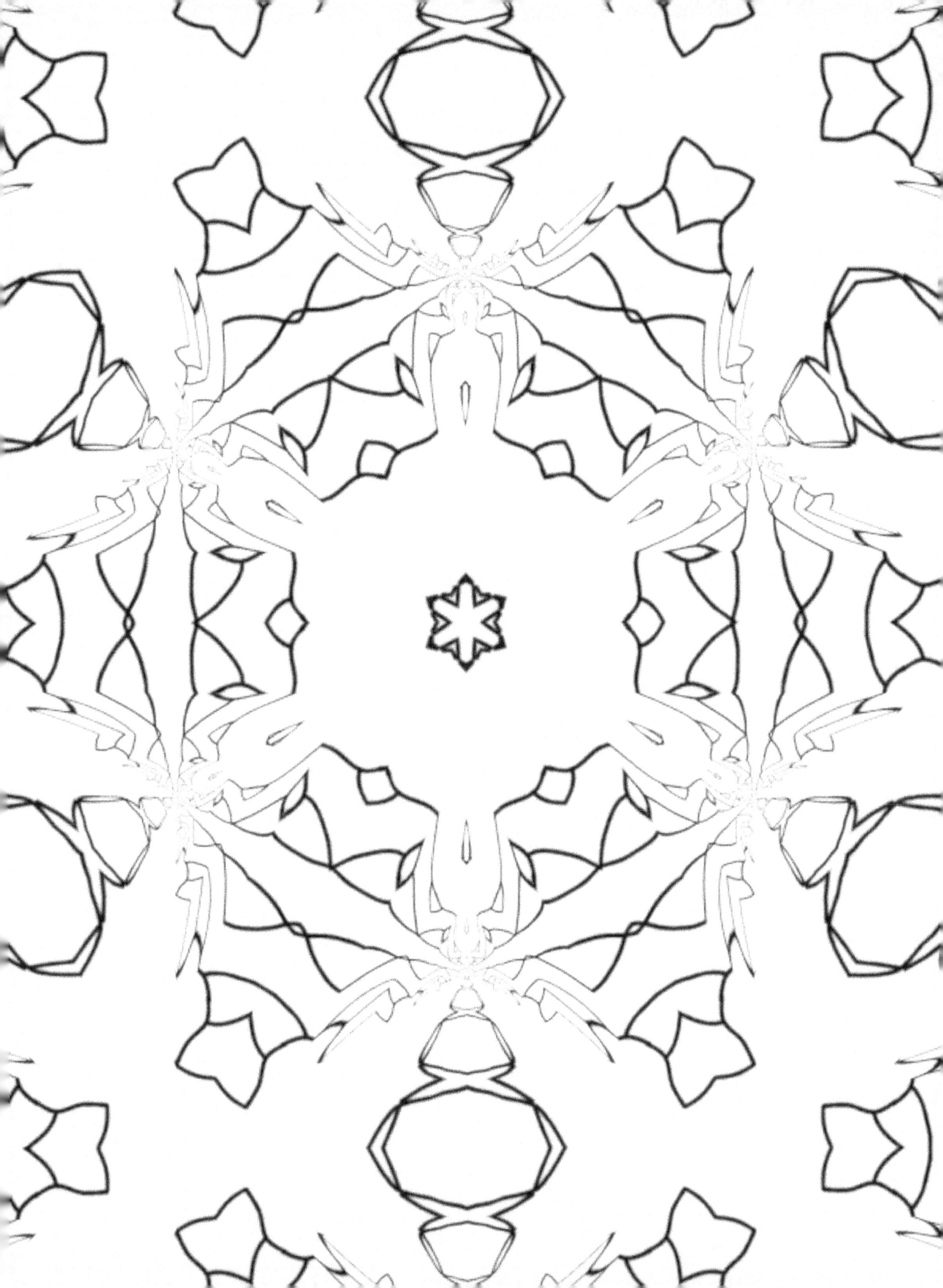

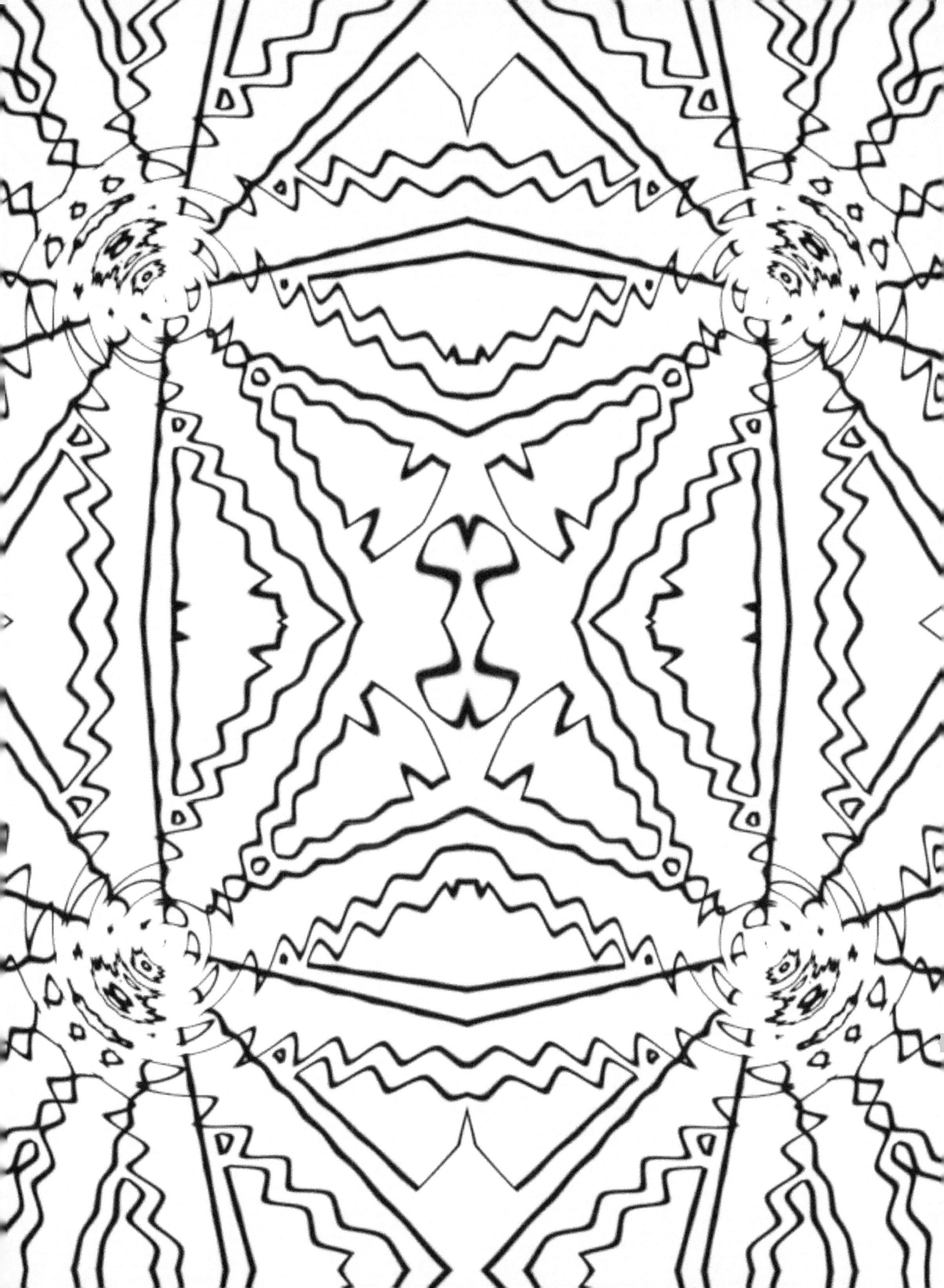

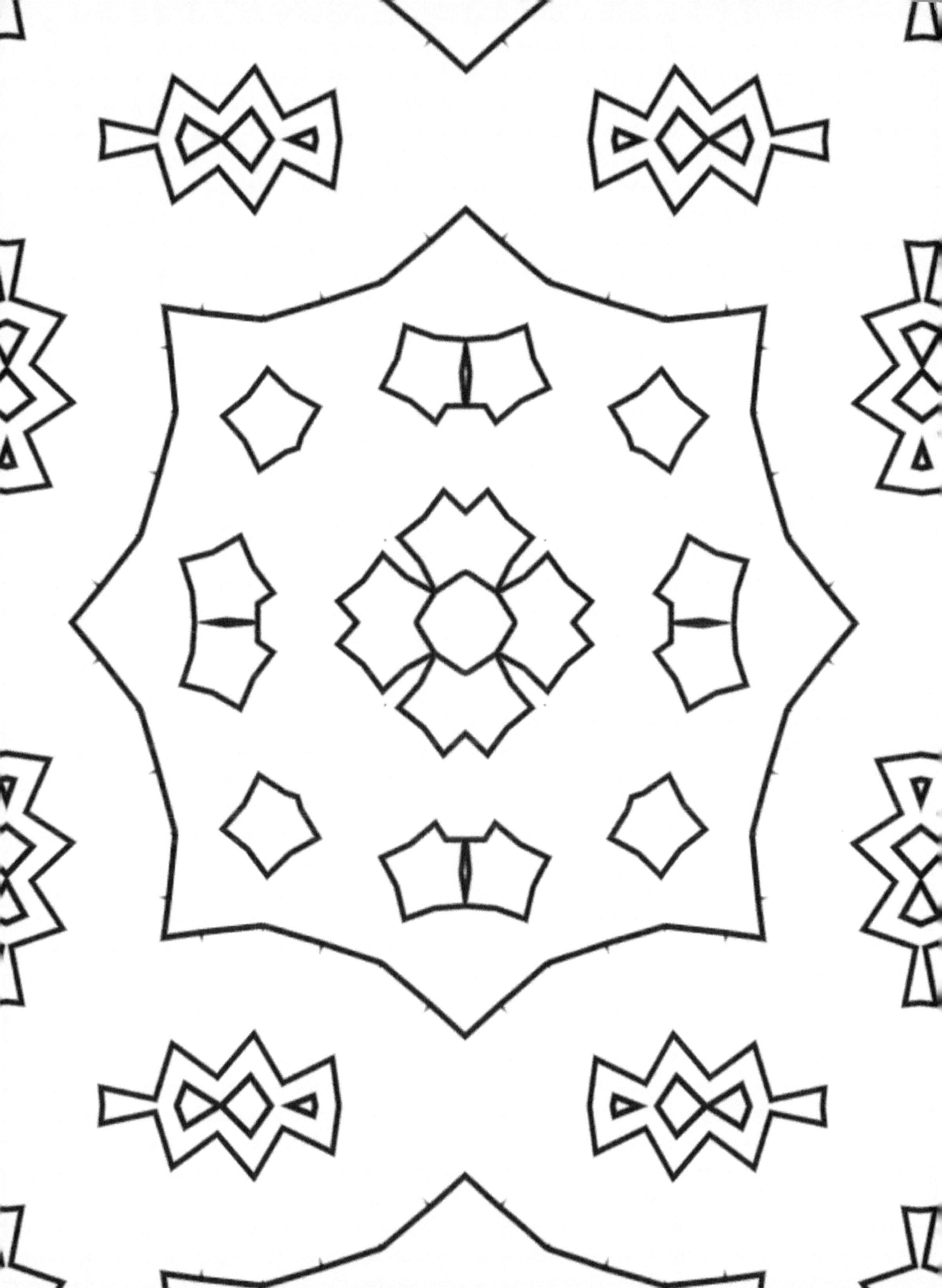

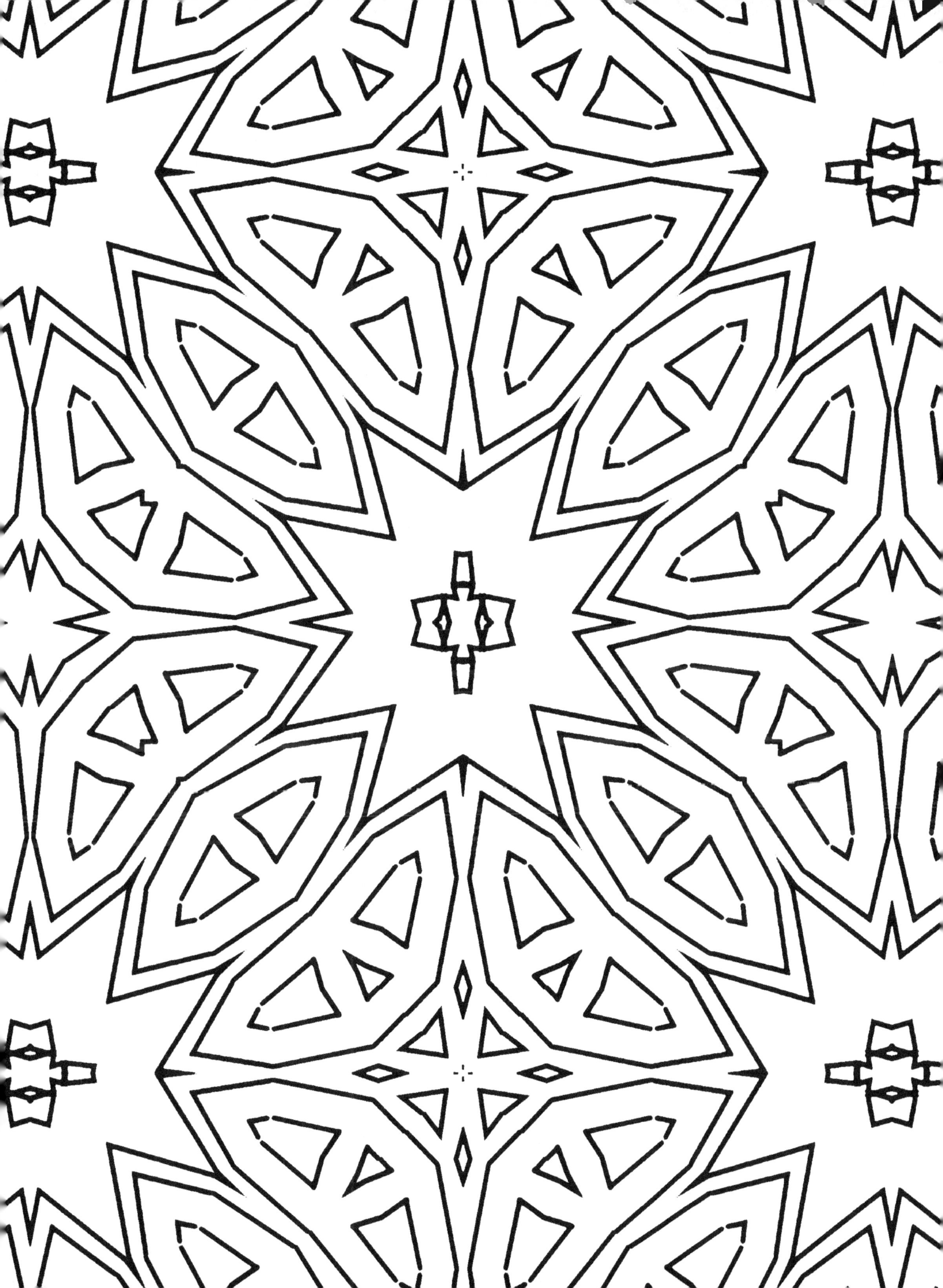

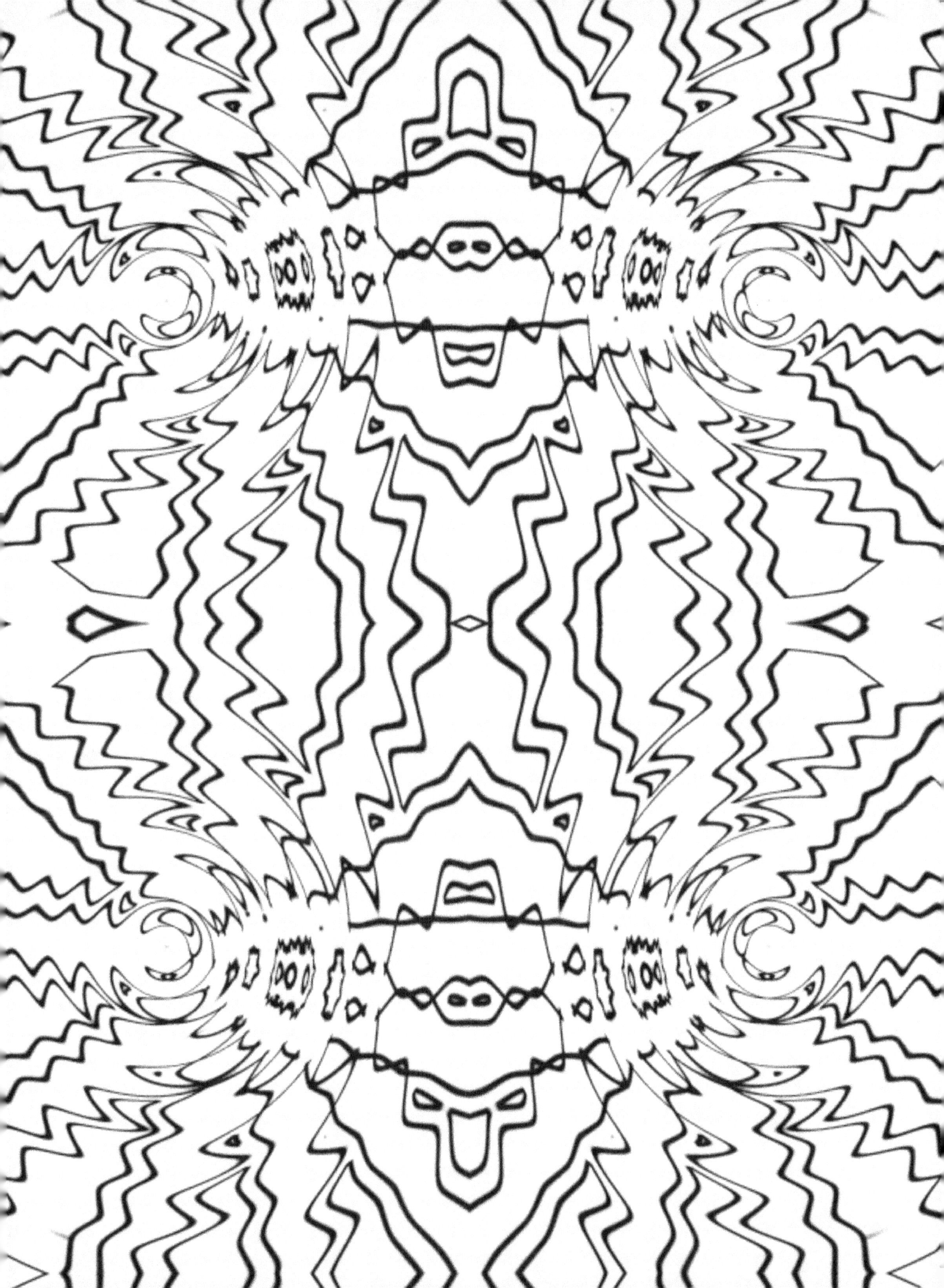

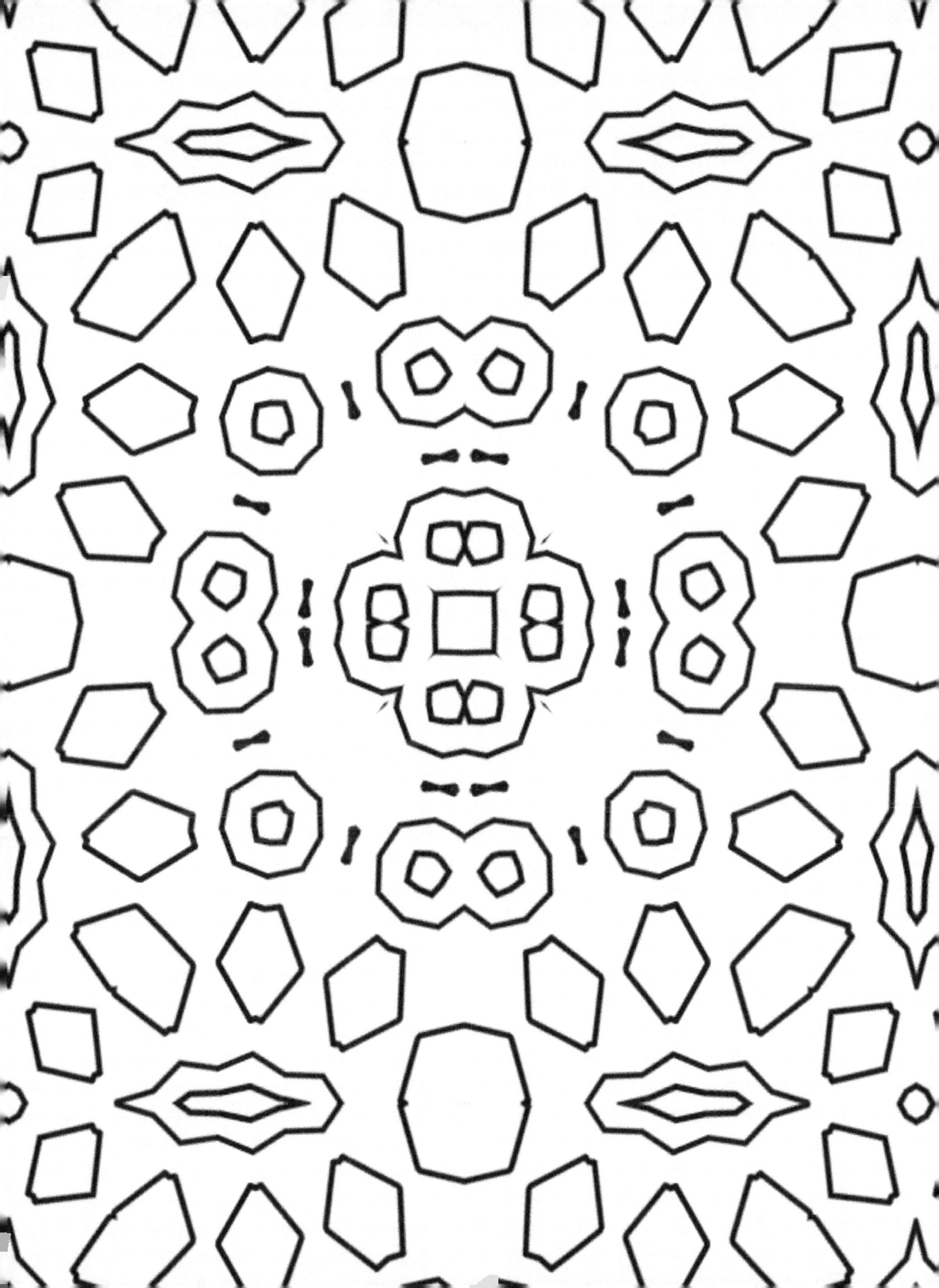

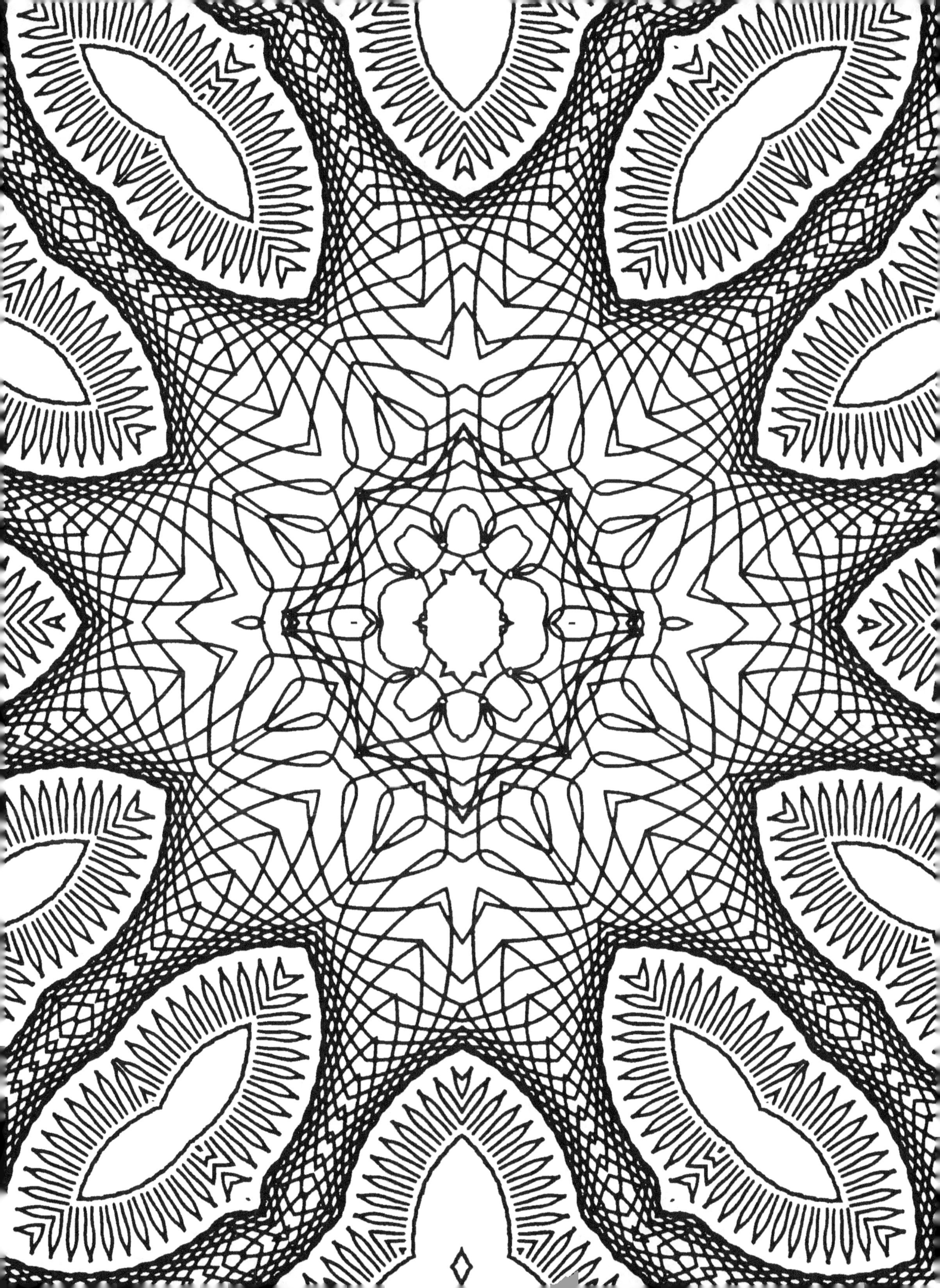

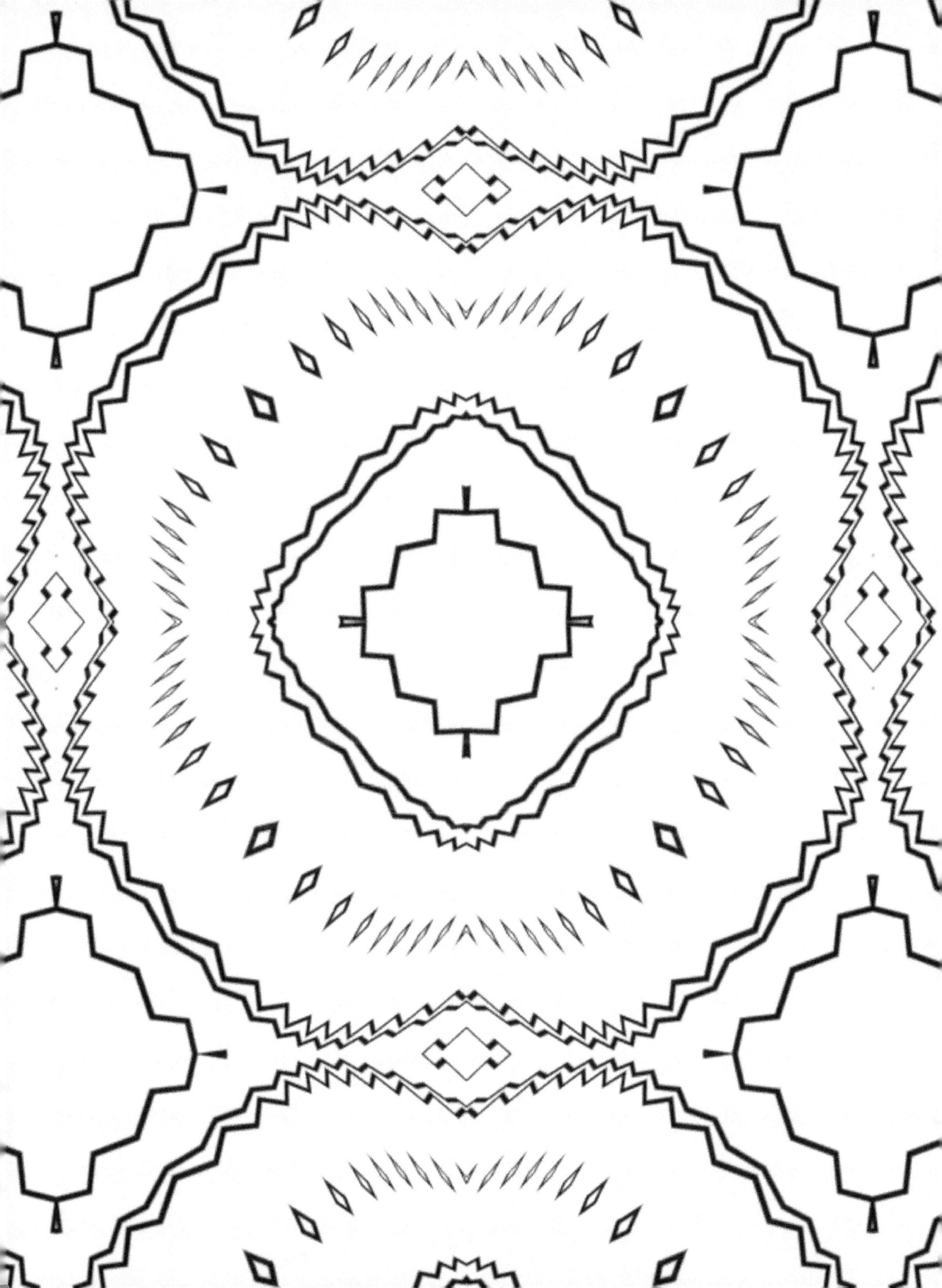

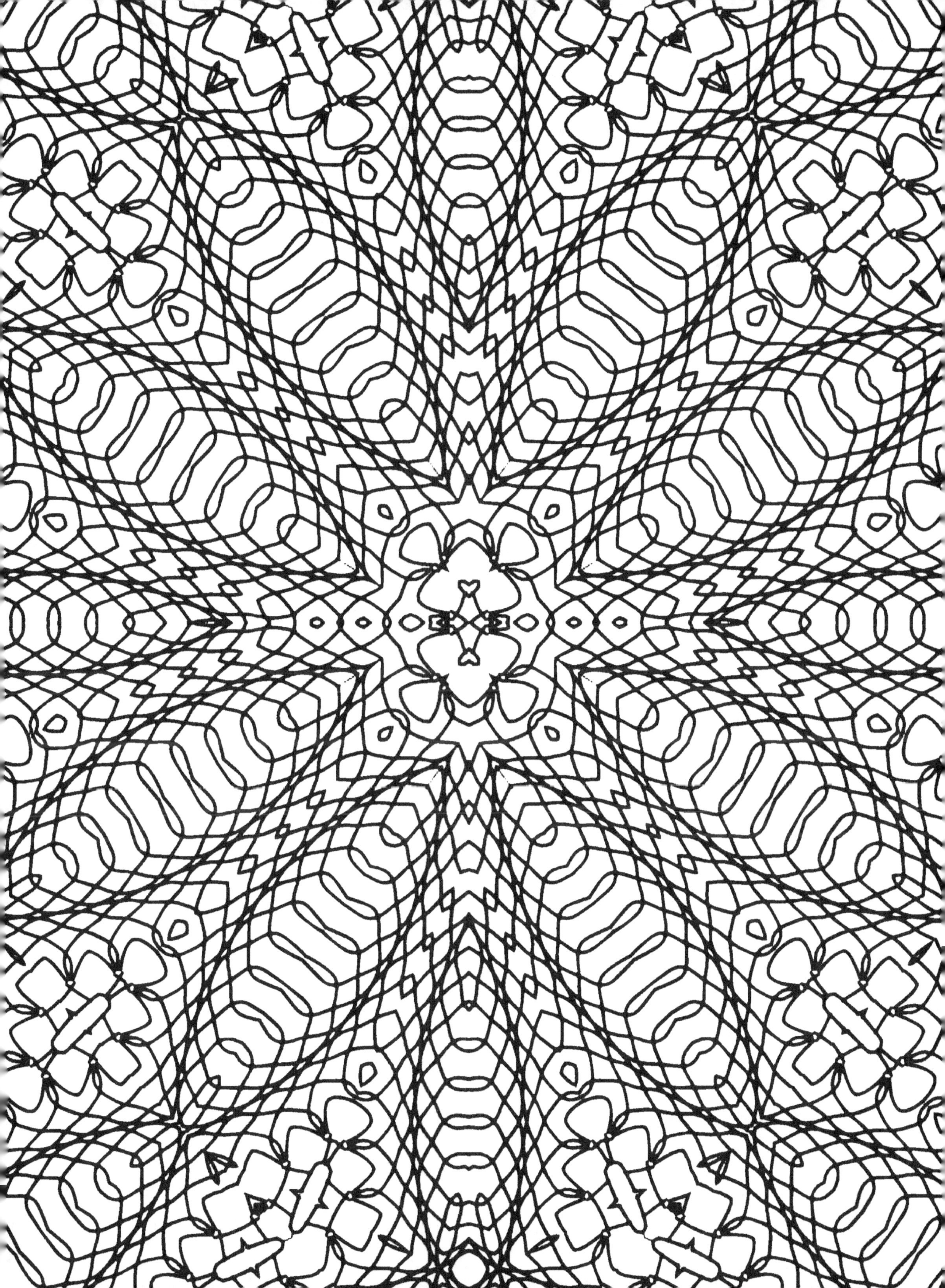

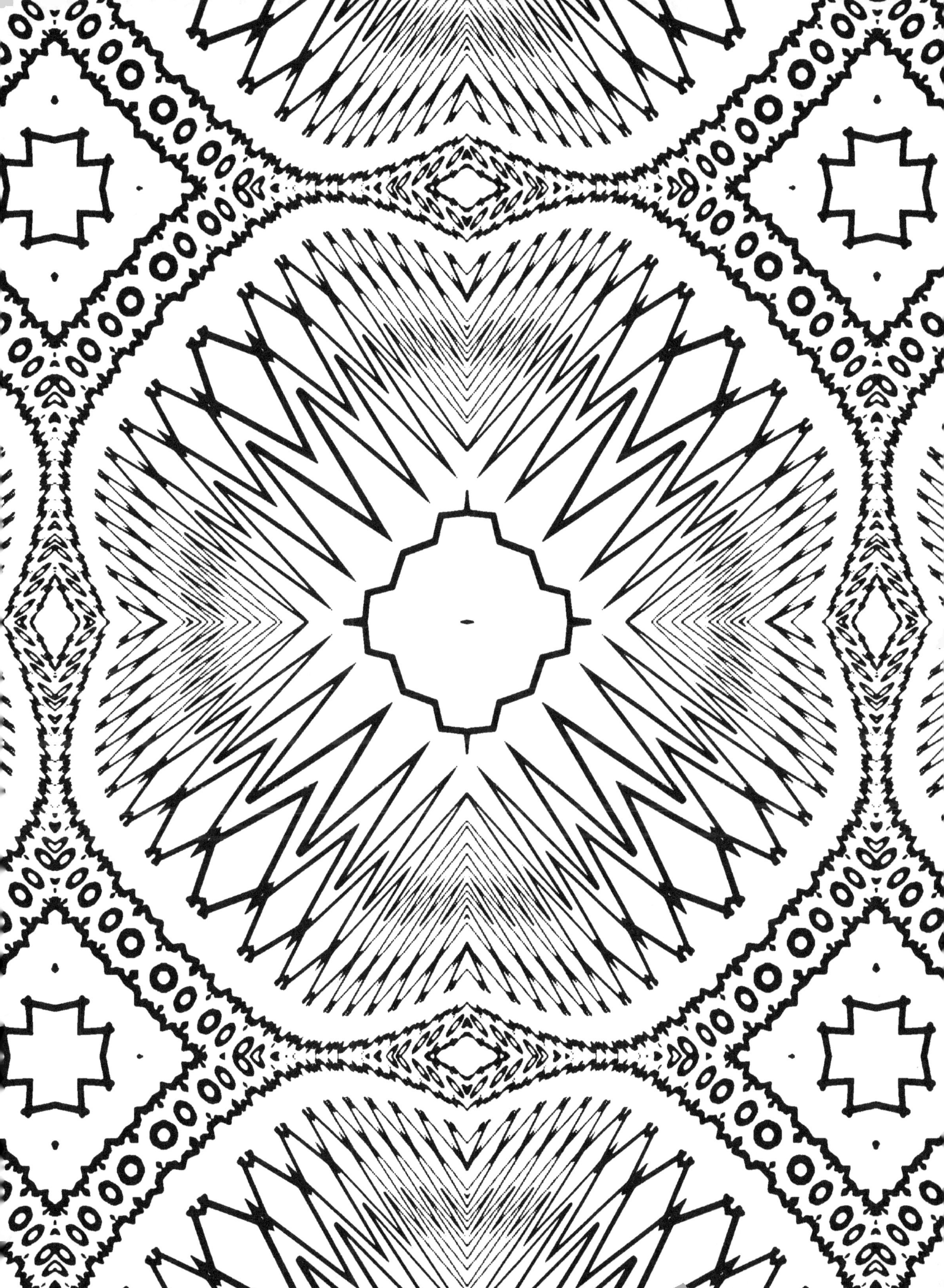

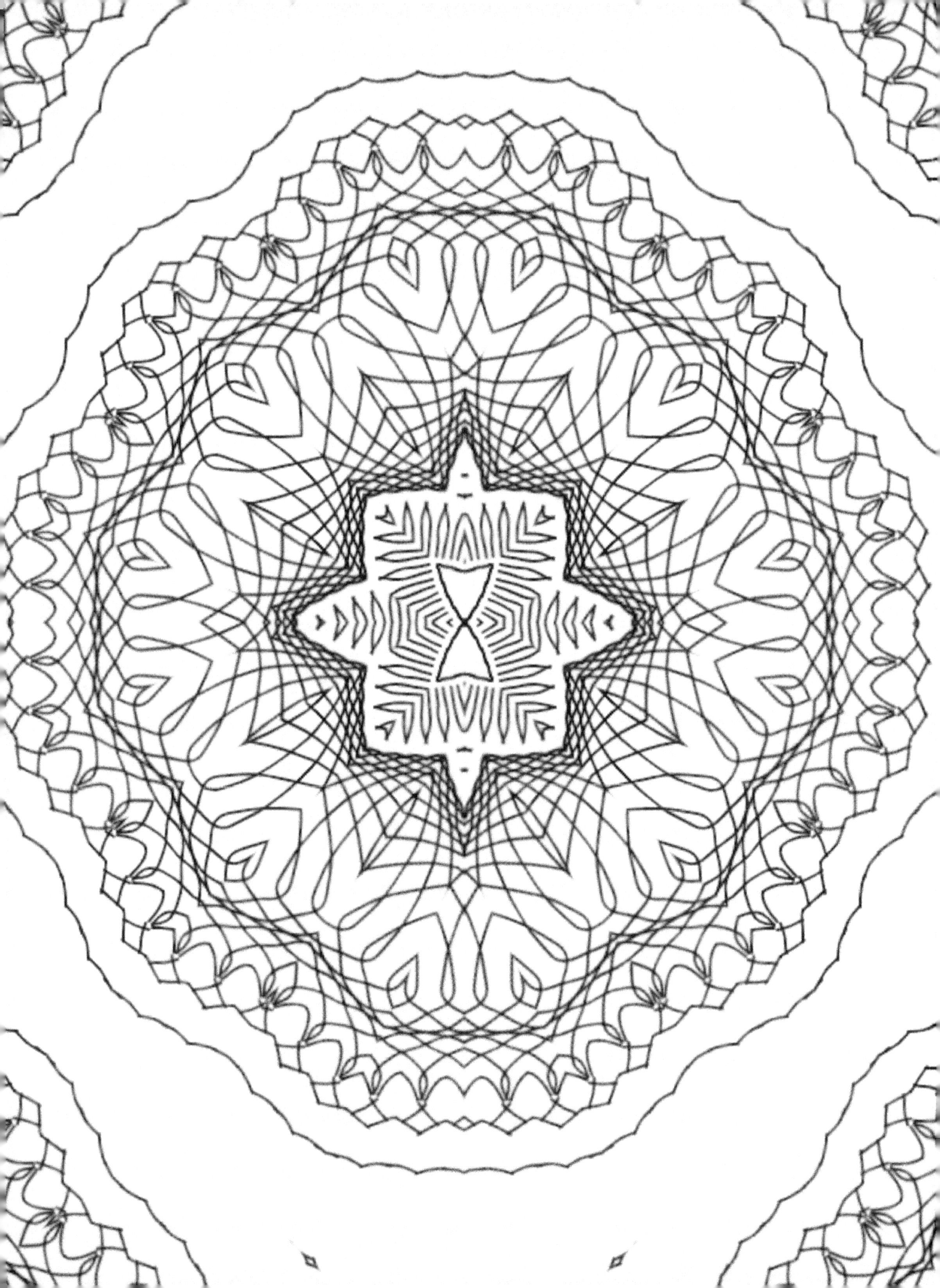

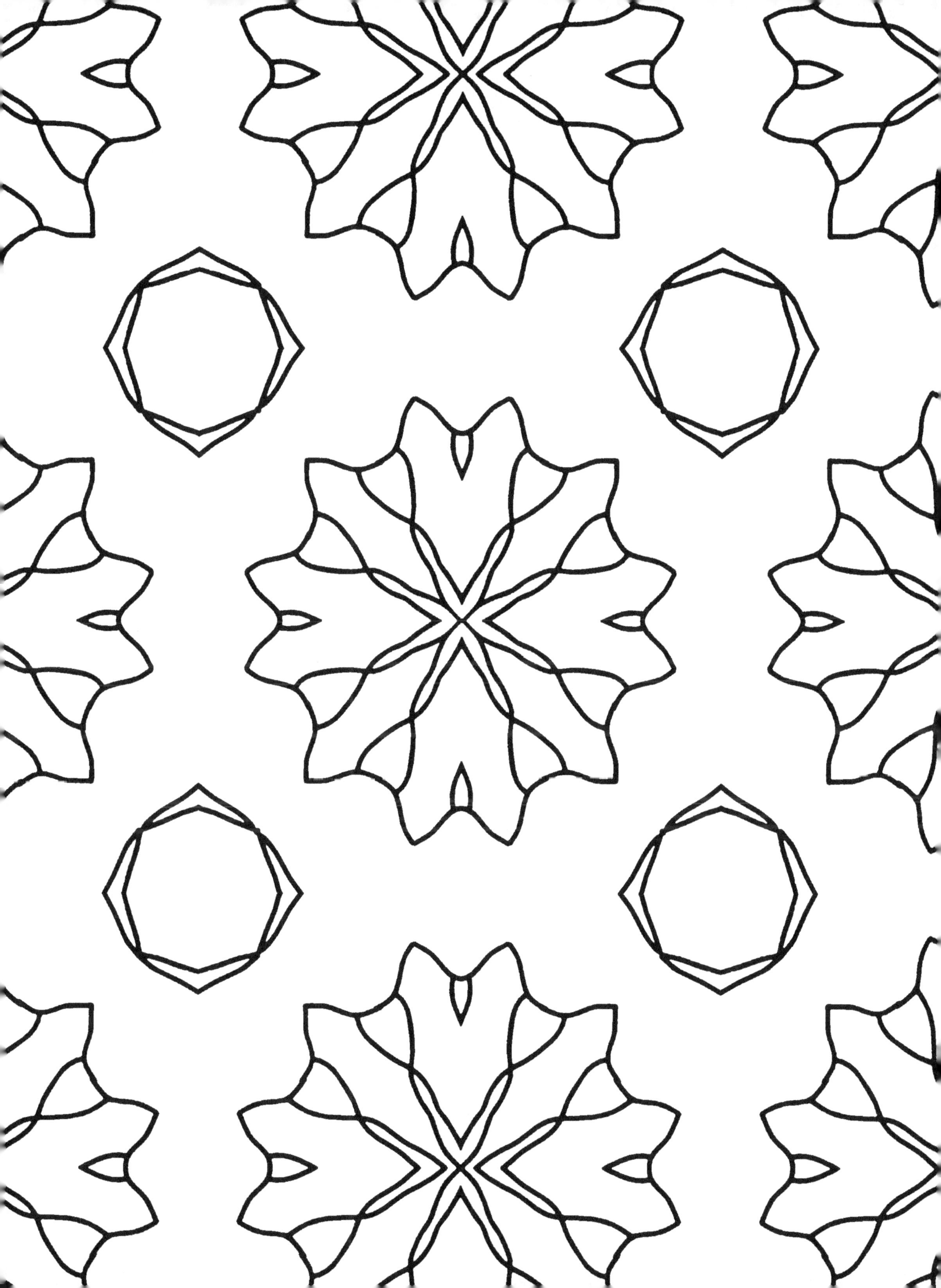